POSTCOLONIAL SITUATION IN THE NOVELS OF

V.S. NAIPAUL

POSTCOLONIAL SITUATION IN THE NOVELS OF V.S. NAIPAUL

Champa Rao Mohan

ATLANTIC

PUBLISHERS & DISTRIBUTORS (P) LTD

Published by

ATLANTIC

PUBLISHERS & DISTRIBUTORS (P) LTD

7/22, Ansari Road, Darya Ganj,
New Delhi-110002
Phones : +91-11-40775252, 23273880, 23275880, 23280451
Fax : +91-11-23285873
Web : www.atlanticbooks.com
E-mail : orders@atlanticbooks.com

Branch Office
5, Nallathambi Street, Wallajah Road,
Chennai-600002
Phones : +91-44-64611085, 32413319
E-mail : chennai@atlanticbooks.com

Printed in India at Nice Printing Press, A-33/3A, Site-IV,
Industrial Area, Sahibabad, Ghaziabad, U.P.

PREFACE

Fragmentation, alienation and disorder are terms often applied in defining the experience of the emergent Third World nations of the world. For the last few centuries, the Third World has remained the object of history, the agent being European Imperialism. Needless to say, imperialism has played the key-role in bringing about the fragmentation, alienation and disorder that characterize not only the Third World countries but also the contemporary world in general. In a world that is growing increasingly complex and difficult for the people of the Third World, the quest for relevance is often the spur as well as the subject matter of all literary endeavours, be it creative or critical. This study of V.S. Naipaul's novels has been undertaken as a quest for meaning.

The choice of the author was mainly determined by the curiosity to know more about this Trinidad-born novelist of Indian ancestry and by the fact that Naipaul has established his reputation as a novelist of post-imperial crisis. It was felt that a study of Naipaul's novels would help add to the emerging new perspective to the problems that confront the post-imperial generations and hence would prove to be a fruitful experience. This work attempts to study V.S. Naipaul's novels in the light of the postcolonial experiences embodied in them. Writing from the unique position of being an East Indian in the West Indies, Naipaul has been able to capture the experiences of the colonized in all its psychological depth, by virtue of which he has carved a niche for himself as a novelist of the colonial experience. He employs the novel form as a tool to carry out a social inquiry into the dereliction of postcolonial societies in particular and the post-imperial world in general. He has a deep conviction in the novel form and believes that the novel form by its seeming indirections can make hidden impulses clear.

What makes Naipaul different from his fellow West Indian writers of the colonial experience is the stance he adopts in his role as an interpreter of Postcolonial cultures and societies. He does not adopt the position of a staunch critic of colonialism as one would expect a Third World novelist of the colonial experience to do, but quite on the contrary, dwells on the contradictions and failings of the postcolonial cultures and societies while criticising them for their intellectual and cultural parasitism on the West. At the same time, however, there runs through his novels a poignant awareness of the traumas of the displaced, deracinated people and the problems and paradoxes of Third World societies that still grope for self-definition.

This study, which deals with the presentation of the postcolonial situation in Naipaul's novels, has been limited to cover only those novels that demonstrate an immediate and obvious concern with the former colonized societies. For the same reason the novel *Mr. Stone and the Knights Companion*, which portrays English middle-class life, has been excluded from the discussion. Although Naipaul's output of non-fiction is prolific and closely interlinked to his fiction, yet his non-fictional works have not been taken up for discussion in a direct manner. However, references have been drawn from his non-fictional works wherever considered relevant for the purpose of our discussion. At this point it would be necessary to qualify the term Postcolonial which in the context of this work, would refer not only to the period immediately following the withdrawal of the colonial powers from the colonies, but would encompass a much wider range of interaction and experience beginning from the very first moment of colonial contact and extending much beyond the end of formal political control. Moreover, while dealing with the novels of a versatile and creative genius like Naipaul, it becomes difficult to restrict oneself only to the novels. Therefore, keeping in mind their thematic significance, the title story of *A Flag on the Island* and *In a Free State* have been included in the discussion, even though the first is closer in form to the novella, and the second is a blend of different genres. Of the remaining three fictional works of Naipaul, *The Enigma of Arrival* and *A Way in the World* have been excluded from the scope of this study as they happen to be mainly autobiographical in nature and do not portray colonized societies directly, while *Half of Life*, Naipaul's latest novel, has not been taken up for discussion as it was published after the manuscript of this book was completed.

Since the purpose of this study is to focus on the problems of the former colonized people both during colonization and after formal decolonization as portrayed in Naipaul's novels, an attempt has been made to approach the novels primarily from the point of view of the themes, while at the same time attempting to maintain their chronological order. As the study focuses on different aspects of cultural colonization, it has also been found necessary to enter into the field of European social anthropology, a discipline which came into existence and was nurtured within the colonial power structure. This study has benefited from the work of those social anthropologists who have shown how anthropological knowledge was put to the use of the colonial mission.

It is a pleasure to record my indebtedness to all the people and institutions that have made this work possible. I am immensely grateful to my teacher and supervisor, Dr. Udayon Misra, Professor in the Department of English, Dibrugarh University, without whose invaluable guidance this work would not have been possible. I owe a lot to my teacher Dr. (Ms) Tilottoma Misra, Professor in the Department of English, for taking a keen interest in my work and helping me in every possible way. I am indebted to the faculty members of the English Department, Dibrugarh University for their encouragement. I extend my thanks to Mr. S.S. Prabhakar of Ramesh Mohan Library, Hyderabad for his help in locating reference material.

I am indebted to Professor C.D. Narasimhaiah for allowing me to use his reputed library "Dhvanyaloka" at Mysore.

I extend my thanks to the librarians and staff members of the National Library and British Council Library, Kolkata; Ramesh Mohan Library and American Studies Research Centre, Hyderabad; British Council Library and Central Library of Jawaharlal Nehru University, New Delhi and the Central Library of Dibrugarh University for their help in locating reference material.

Finally, I convey my sincere thanks to the University Grants Commission for providing financial support to the work.

CHAMPA RAO MOHAN

Abbreviations

The following abbreviations have been used for the titles of V.S. Naipaul's books:

The Mystic Masseur	*Masseur*
The Suffrage of Elvira	*Suffrage*
Miguel Street	*Street*
A House for Mr. Biswas	*House*
The Middle Passage	*Passage*
Mr. Stone and the Knights Companion	*Mr. Stone*
An Area of Darkness	*Area*
The Mimic Men	*Mimic*
A Flag on the Island	*Flag*
In a Free State	*State*
The Overcrowded Barracoon and other Articles	*Barracoon*
A Bend in the River	*Bend*
The Return of Eva Peron with the Killings in Trinidad	*Return*
Finding the Centre	*Centre*

CONTENTS

1

Introduction

> This [modern] colonialism colonizes minds in addition to bodies and it releases forces within the colonized societies to alter their cultural priorities once for all. In the process it helps generalize the concept of the modern West from a geographical and temporal entity to a psychological category. The West is now everywhere, within the West and outside, in structures and in minds.[1]
>
> —*Ashis Nandy*

The era of imperialism has finally passed and today most of the colonies have attained an independent status. Yet, an examination of these developing nations of the Third World brings to light diverse problems that clearly are a legacy of imperialism. The damage done to the economy of these countries is undoubtedly, immense, but imperialism has to answer for damages of a graver, more overwhelming nature like the damage done to the psyche of the colonized people, through the subtle process of cultural colonization. Today, the Third World countries are grappling with the dual problem of regaining their economic stability disrupted during colonial rule as well as rediscovering their potential for political, social and cultural growth curbed under the colonial system. In his book entitled *The Third World Reassessed,* Elbaki Hermassi throws light on the exact nature of the crisis that grips the Third World countries when he says that the Third World crisis is neither purely political nor exclusively economic for "the political and economic are only aspects of a larger crisis that is at the heart civilizational."[2] For a people whose history and culture have been denigrated and themselves labelled as inferior, the gravity of the problem could not but have assumed such proportions.

Colonialism has been a recurrent and widespread feature of human history. The Roman Empire can be traced back to as early as the second century A.D. World history records many more empires like the Inca, Aztec, Ottoman and the Chinese, to name only some of them. In fact, the Chinese Empire was even larger than the modern European Empires. However, since these empires were pre-capitalist, their colonial practices were limited to the extraction of tributes, goods and wealth from the countries they conquered. European colonialism, on the other hand, was established alongside capitalism and had a much more drastic effect on its colonies. As Ania Loomba writes, "it restructured the economies of the latter [colonized countries] drawing them into a complex relationship with their own, so that there was a flow of human and natural resources between colonised and colonial countries."[3] Therefore no part of the globe remains untouched by it. Economic exploitation happens to be the least significant feature of the larger crises that are the aftermath of the colonial encounter. Domination being the essence of imperialism, it was the colonizers who always had the upperhand in the colonies. Every sphere of the lives of the subjugated people, beginning from what they grew to whom they worshipped, was regulated by the colonizers. The Europeans even did it with a sense of martyrdom. They projected themselves as martyrs dedicated to the great cause of spreading the light of their "superior civilization" among the "backward peoples" of the world.

Even though we believe, if only for a moment, in the altruistic intentions of the colonizers, the basic fact still remains unpalatable—that the Europeans considered all other civilizations as backward and inferior when compared to their own and sought to impose their own ways on those they colonized. It is significant that the idea of the civilizing mission came to be stressed at the end of the eighteenth century when questions were being raised in England about the economic feasibility of maintaining its overseas territories and it was claimed that economic viability could be achieved indirectly through the civilizing mission, for, "the savage no sooner becomes ashamed of his nakedness, than the loom is ready to clothe him" (qtd. in Jenny Sharpe: 141). It is apparent, therefore, that the civilizing mission was a "human-making project of inculcating Western tastes and values"[4] in the indigenous population with the motive of promoting the colonizing nation's economic interests. To create a market for English broadcloth among the so called savages, it was first necessary to make them view their nakedness through the perspective of Western cultural norms of decency.

The roots of the patronizing attitude of the Europeans towards non-Western societies can be traced back to the seventeenth century when the medieval concept of the "Chain of Being" became dynamic and came to be conceived as a ladder up which the higher forms of life had ascended through time. When the notion of progress became attached to human societies, there was a tendency among Western scholars and scientists to rank and order them. The scale against which other cultures came to be assessed was obviously the European culture, which was assumed to be the highest in the hierarchy. Ranked on the basis of their difference from the European culture, the cultures that came lowest in the hierarchy were labelled as "savages." In the nineteenth century, when Charles Darwin propounded his theory of evolution, Western social scientists borrowed Darwin's ideas and designed their doctrine of "Social Darwinism" to legitimise their stand and maintain the status quo.[5] Not only that, the doctrine of Social Darwinism was itself given twists and turns when it conflicted with their own religious beliefs. Social Darwinists interpreted cultural differences between Western and non-Western societies as being the result of varying rates of progress up the evolutionary ladder. But religious orthodoxy was not prepared to accept the idea that civilized societies had developed gradually from a primitive state comparable to that of the savages. This was because according to the biblical account of creation, God created man in his own image. If the theory of cultural evolution was accepted, God's image would come under question. To avoid this, the biblical scholars known as the "degenerationists" argued that though originally all humans were created in the perfect image of God, a degeneration had set in for some reason, as a result of which a part of humanity had fallen into a state of savagery.

In the nineteenth century, the interest in other societies

spurred by the age of discovery emerged as a developing discipline. Anthropological studies of traditional societies were undertaken wherein the social and political institutions of these societies were compared to Western ones. Such studies only served to verify imperialistic prejudices because of the comparative method and the ethnocentric point of view adopted by the cultural anthropologists of the time. The basic assumption of ethnocentrism, that one's own culture is preferred to all others, was biased.[6] What these anthropologists failed to see was, that culture is a relative term and springs from the day to day requirements of the people which are not uniform, so that culture varies from people to people. For instance, the technique for fur coats could only have been developed by the people living in the Arctic because of their need to protect themselves from the bitter cold of the Arctic region.

The concept of cultural relativism introduced by the German-born Franz Boas, did away with the correlation between culture and race, that Western social scientists had been trying to establish. Boas pointed out that the history of each cultural group is distinct and cannot be ranked against another culture with a different history. It became clear that cultures can neither be compared nor ranked by reference to any one standard because an ideal model, which could serve as the scale for such evaluations did not exist.

In fact, the very application of the principles of biological evolution to the analysis of cultural change is questionable at the basic level of the mechanics that govern the two kinds of changes—genetic mutations occur at random while cultural innovations are introduced to answer specific needs, and are largely within human control. It is surprising that the major role played by the human brain in the growth of culture could thus have been overlooked.[7] Darwin himself never meant his theory of evolution to be applied to social change. "Social Darwinism" was only a misapplication of his theory. The transfer of Darwin's evolutionary scheme to social evolution paved the way for ethnocentric doctrines which assumed the superiority of Western societies and provided the imperialists with a pretext for justifying colonialism. Colonialism was re-interpreted in benevolent terms, as a way of helping backward and inferior non-Western societies survive in the face of impending extinction because they lacked the technological capabilities to combat the forces of evolution operating against them.

It is apparent that colonialism was a lot more than mere military conquest. It was, as Nicholas B. Dirks puts it, "a cultural project of control,"[8] that displaced traditional cultures and left a deep scar on the psyche of the colonized people, who found themselves in the excruciating state of betweenity. For not only were they denied of their own culture, but were given only a partial admittance into the mother culture. Acculturation studies, like the one done by Margaret Mead, about the plains Indian people in contact with white society, clearly reveals that "while the Indians were encouraged to adopt the white people's ways, at the same time they were prevented by white prejudice from participating in joint cultural ventures.[9]

The process of cultural colonization was similar in all colonies. It was effected in a planned and systematic manner, through two important institutions: the school and the church. These institutions played a major role in the suffusion of Western cultural values into the fabric of the existing traditional cultures. The curriculum introduced in the colonial schools was completely Europeanized in the sense that the information diffused through it mainly pertained to European geography, history and literature. On the other hand the church dispatched missionaries to the newly annexed lands, motivated by the urge to spread Christianity by converting "non-believers." Though the missionaries were not prompted by selfish interests, they failed to realise that those whom they considered non-believers had their own belief system, which was equally sacred to them. The missionaries were used by the colonizers to "tame" the so-called savages.

The colonizers were well aware that for the process of cultural colonization to become a possibility, it was first important to make the colonized receptive to Western cultural influences. The grounds for cultural colonization was prepared through the propagation of myths about the colonized masses that projected them in the most unfavourable light. These myths instilled a feeling of inferiority in the minds of the colonized and psychologically conditioned them for the process which the Europeans chose to call "modernization." Albert Memmi gives a succinct analysis of the colonized mind when he observes:

> Constantly confronted with this image of himself, set forth and imposed on all institutions and in every human contact, how could the colonized help reacting to his portrait.... The accusation disturbs him and worries him even more because he admires and fears his powerful accuser. "Is he not partially right?" he mutters. "Are we not all a little guilty after all? Lazy, because we have so many idlers? Timid, because we let ourselves be oppressed." Willfully created and spread by the colonizer, this mythical and degrading portrait ends up by being accepted and lived with to a certain extent by the colonized. It thus acquires a certain amount of reality and contributes to the true portrait of the colonized.[10]

With the minds of the colonized people thus attuned, the process of cultural colonization became easier. Antonio Gramsci's concept of hegemony clearly shows that the colonizers maintained their cultural dominance over the peripheries not only by force but also by creating willing victims through the medium of ideology. In Gramsci's view ideologies "create the terrain on which men move" (qtd. in Loomba: 30).

Sushanta Goonatilake's extensive study on cultural colonization reveals that cultural colonization first occurred in the strata allied to the colonial presence and later percolated downwards socially, through acts of imitation as well as the spread of education.[11] The kind of education provided under colonial tutelage involved the passing of examinations largely through the exercise of memory functions and thus had no significant relation to actual life. The middle class was a new social strata created during imperial rule. A product of Western education, the middle class filled the important posts in the colonies, but could not form a critical intelligentsia. The middle class played a key role in absorbing and transmitting the colonial culture. However, resistance to colonial culture also came from the elite class. It happened when the elites, on coming into direct contact with the colonial power in the metropolis realized the social and cultural facts of colonization. Fanon, Nehru, Gandhi and Cabral came from the upper strata of the colonized nations. It was through the medium of literature that the Third World intellectuals mobilized the subjugated people to rise up against and overthrow colonial domination.

The relation between literature and the historical phenomenon of imperialism has been a long and intimate one. In fact, literature played the key role in validating imperial rule. For long, it served as an arena in which the main issues related to imperialism were "reflected, contested and even for a time decided."[12] The imperialists harnessed the services of literature for the two-fold purpose of perpetuating Western culture and ideology in the colonies as well as exerting an energising influence on their own people back home. While discussing this aspect, Martin Green reveals that the adventure tales that formed the light reading of English men for two hundred years and more after *Robinson Crusoe* were, in fact, the "energising myths of English imperialism," meant to charge "England's will with the energy to go out into the world and explore, conquer, and rule."[13] Even victorian literature was infused with imperial ideas of race pride and national prowess. The culmination was reached when Kipling appeared on the scene. He glorified imperialism because he deeply believed in the civilizing mission and came to be regarded as "the greatest apostle of imperialism of his time."[14] On the other hand, even when imperialism was at its height and appeared unassailable, the intellectuals of the Third World were gradually preparing the ground to overthrow it with the help of those very ideas which the imperialistic process had initiated. Initially of course the colonized people's narratives about the colonial experience were blocked from emerging and hence could not be more than "mere traces in the writing of the time."[15] It was in the early part of the twentieth century, when the power and glory of Empire began to wane, that the monopoly on imperial writing was broken and the colonized elites could articulate their protest against the imperial power, which they did by appropriating the language and literary forms of the colonizers.[16] The early part of the twentieth century was marked by the emergence of colonial nationalist writing which sought to subvert Western cultural hegemony as well as recover and reaffirm the suppressed identity of the colonized subjects. This may be supposed to be the beginning of postcolonial writing in the colonies, which since has been a proliferating area of interest for intellectuals.

Postcolonial literature, concerns itself primarily with the experiences of the former colonized people. Elleke Boehmer defines it as "that which critically scrutinizes the colonial relationship."[17] It gives expression to the colonial experience from the "other's" perspective, which includes all the cultures that were affected by the imperial process. In the context of the Caribbean too, there has been a substantial contribution to postcolonial literature. As Bruce King observes in his introduction to *West Indian Literature*:

> West Indian is one of many English literatures, that began under colonialism and 'emerged' after the Second World War, mostly as a result of the social, political and cultural changes which had started in the late 1930s and which picked up speed during the war and with the ending of Empire. As with other new literatures its development has paralleled the rise of national movements and its themes and subject-matter have often been the problems resulting from colonialism and independence.[18]

V.S. Naipaul is an important West Indian novelist of the colonial experience. As a postcolonial novelist, Naipaul situates his novels in both colonial as well as ex-colonial societies and gives a perceptive account of the complexities inherent to such societies. The major themes that emerge from a reading of his novels are related to the problems of the colonized people: their sense of alienation from the landscapes, their identity crisis, the paradox of freedom and the problem of neocolonialism in the ex-colonies. In the first four novels Naipaul deals exclusively with the colonial society of Trinidad, the island of his nativity, and is preoccupied with the themes of dispossession, homelessness, alienation, mimicry and the search for an authentic selfhood. The characters in these novels are continually in search of an identity and home. In the later novels he emerges as a novelist of post-imperial crisis. His critical, observant eye and his uncompromising commitment to truth lay bare the hard facts about the ex-colonial societies. Naipaul makes it clear that political independence has changed nothing and the imperialist states continue to retain their hold on the former colonies through the newer, more camouflaged methods of neocolonialism. The characters in the later novels are even more lost and insecure than those depicted in the early novels.

Much of Naipaul's writing issues from his personal experience of being a displaced member of a minority race and religion in Trinidad. However, his multiple heritage places him in a position that makes it possible for him to render a detached account of his subjective experiences. Being an Indian by ancestry, Trinidadian by birth and English by intellectual training and residence, Naipaul is indeed a man with a broader perspective.

This of course did pose a difficulty for him when he first ventured into his writing career because, his material was not "sufficiently hallowed by a tradition."[19] He realized that though he could stake a claim on the English language, yet, the English literary tradition with its alien mythology could never be his. Naipaul found a way out of the problem through his father's stories, which provided him with a starting-point. The ambition of becoming a writer was, in the first place, something that had come to him from his father, who followed the occupation of a journalist, which was unusual for a Trinidad Indian of his generation. His father's stories opened up an exciting world to Naipaul, who went to them as to memorials of a heroic time he had missed. In a way the stories compensated for Naipaul's lack of tradition. Having found a model for his work, Naipaul set about establishing his home identity by ordering his experiences through his writing. This was finally accomplished in his fourth novel, *A House for Mr. Biswas*.[20] Naipaul now turned his attention to other "half made" societies and took to travel writing, which resulted in *The Middle Passage*,[21] his first travel book. This book did not find a favourable response in the West Indies because of Naipaul's scathing criticism of the West Indies. *Passage* was followed by more travelogues based on Naipaul's travels to India, Africa, the Islamic world and South America. The non-fictional works are interspersed with novels which render a fictional account of his travels to other Caribbean islands and Africa. In his later novels, *The Mimic Men,*[22] *Guerrillas*[23] and "*A Bend in the River*[24] as well as in his novellas contained in *A Flag on the Island*[25] and *In a Free State,*[26] Naipaul's themes acquire a universality as he enters other states of minds and cultures to take note of the fact that fragmentation and alienation happen to be the universal predicament of man in the present day world.

In Naipaul's vision of the world, pessimism may be said to be a central strain, while his commitment to truth is uncompromising. As his vision matures, it becomes increasingly pessimistic with his own growing sense of disillusionment. As an observer and interpreter of the ex-colonies, especially, he is unsparingly critical and exposes the inadequacies of such societies, which he believes to be the outcome of the unconscious acceptance of the norms and values of the colonizing culture. Naipaul's early novels happen to be the liveliest of all his novels. Yet, one can sense the pain and distress even in the midst of laughter. Naipaul himself acknowledges the fact in an interview, when he says: "Even my funniest novels were all begun in the blackest of moods, out of a sense of personal anguish and despair...."[27] It is the personal nature of the anguish experienced by him that defines his attitude and sets the tone of all Naipaul's novels.

A third generation Indian in Trinidad, Naipaul was never at ease with his identity as a Trinidadian. When he was still in the fourth form, he had inscribed his determination to leave Trinidad within five years, in the end paper of his *Kennedy's Revised Latin Primer.* He actually left after six years, when he won a government scholarship and opted to study English at Oxford. Naipaul's rejection of his birthplace had something to do with the nature of the Trinidadian society itself. It was in his own words, "unimportant, uncreative [and] cynical."[28] The Trinidadian society was an immigrant society consisting of "various races, religion and cliques."[29] The only binding factor was common residence, which is hardly enough to generate the feeling of oneness which forms the basis of a community. The society of Trinidad was a fragmented one, comprising of heterogeneous people, whose presence in the island was purely an accident of history. In *Passage,* commenting on the manufactured nature of West Indian societies Naipaul observes: "The West Indian colonial situation is unique because the West Indies, in all their racial and social complexity, are so completely a creation of Empire that the withdrawal of Empire is almost without meaning."[30] In the absence of a common West Indian identity nationalism was impossible. Moreover, there was not even any anti-imperialistic feelings among the Trinidadians. On the contrary, it was rather their "Britishness," their "belonging to the British Empire" that gave them a sense of identity.[31]

The colonial history of the West Indies has been a brutal one. It involved the near decimation of the aboriginal inhabitants and the enslaving of another race—the Negroes. The Negroes, who were brought to the West Indies as slaves are perhaps the worst affected victims of colonialism. Writing about the effect of slavery on the West Indian Negroes, Naipaul observes that the greatest damage done to the Negro by slavery was that it taught him "self contempt."[32] Naipaul further writes that slavery "set him the ideals of white civilization and made him despise every other."[33] These West Indian Negroes born outside Africa became completely oblivious of their African ancestry. Captured as slaves from different parts of the country, the Negroes belonged to different tribes, each of which had a distinct language and culture. After being brought to the West Indies, tribes and even families were deliberately broken up and dispersed by the colonizing powers, so as to prevent the formation of revolutionary groups.[34] They were not even allowed to retain their traditional cultures. In the absence of a common language and tradition the Negroes were unable to form a single unified identity. With the imposition of the colonizing culture, these West Indian Negroes of African origin came to acquire the language, religion and even the attitudes of the Europeans. Ironically, they even shared the Europeans' contempt for the Africans. This is clearly evident in Naipaul's quotation from Trollope in *Passage*:

> The West Indian Negro knows nothing of Africa except that it is a term of reproach. If African immigrants are put to work on the same estate with him, he will not eat

> with them, or drink with them, or walk with them. He will hardly work beside them, and regards himself as a creature immeasurably the superior of the newcomer (qtd. in Naipaul: 71).

The East Indians' colonial experience, on the other hand, differed qualitatively from that of the Negroes. They arrived on the West Indian scene much later and had the background of a well-established civilization. Besides, most of the East Indians of Trinidad, having migrated from the Indian province of Bihar and Uttar Pradesh, shared a common language and tradition. They were thus able to maintain a distinct identity. From the very beginning, the governing power too adopted a policy of separation and division of the two major racial groups: the Negroes and the East Indians. This is evident in the fact that separate schools were established for them.[35] Owing to their geographical separation in the villages, the East Indians hardly came into contact with the outside world and were culturally insular. However, for the generations born in exile, India lost the sense of reality that it had conveyed to their ancestors. For these later generations India became a mythical ancestral land about which they knew little besides what they had been told. The impact of urbanization gradually exposed the later generations of East Indians to the influence of the dominant Creole culture in Port of Spain and the insularity of the Indians was broken into. Thereafter followed the painful process of acculturation. Nevertheless, unlike the Negroes who completely forgot Africa, the East Indians "never lost pride in their origins"[36] and were saved from the self-contempt to which the Negroes had fallen victims. As Naipaul points out in *Finding the Centre,*[37] it was the life of the clan that gave the East Indians, "a caste certainty, a high sense of the self."[38]

The East Indians form an important element in the population of Trinidad. Yet, this section of the society remained neglected in the West Indian literature for a long time. Gerald Moore, writing about the development of West Indian writing recognizes Naipaul as the first truly representative writer of the East Indians, in the following words:

> But in all this opening of a new region for the novelist and reader, the great East Indian section of people,

> especially strong in Trinidad, has largely remained submerged. The new writers, for the main part black or coloured, have been content to give us such figures as Jagadir, the Indian clerk in *A Morning at the Office*, who is the most genuinely outcast person in the book. What is his world? What are the values, culture, daily life of his people? We have no inkling until the arrival of V.S. Naipaul. In two remarkable novels he has given us the very smell, taste and tempo of life in the Indian locations of Trinidad.[39]

Naipaul being an East Indian himself speaks largely from his own childhood memories and is able to render a more accurate and comprehensive picture of what was to him a lived experience. In his early novels that form the Trinidad tetralogy—*The Mystic Masseur*,[40] *The Suffrage of Elvira*,[41] *Miguel Street*[42] and *A House for Mr. Biswas*,[43] Naipaul deals predominantly with the East Indian experience in the West Indies. He presents a poignant picture of the East Indians struggling to preserve their identity in an alien environment, but ultimately succumbing to the influence of the dominating culture. The compromises that these Indians have to make in order to come to terms with the alien environment and forge an identity for themselves, form a long and painful process, which is touchingly retold by Naipaul. Naipaul, equally, exposes the inadequacies of his society, but his tone is sympathetic. He understands the unique predicament of immigrant colonial societies and in *The Overcrowded Baracoon*,[44] he accepts the fact that the Indians of Trinidad are no longer of Asia, but a part of the New world:

> Immigrants are people on their own. They cannot be judged by the standards of their older culture. Culture is like language, ever developing. There is no right and wrong; no purity from which there is decline. Usage sanctions everything.[45]

While Naipaul's view about culture is progressive, there is at the same time a regret for the passing away of the old order. In *An Area of Darkness*[46] he confesses: "The thought of the decay of the old customs and reverences saddened me."[47] In the first four novels, Naipaul recreates the society of Trinidad and traces the disintegration of the East Indian community.

As the experiences are of an intensely personal nature and are reproduced from the author's own memories, the account is to some extent autobiographical. Many incidents and events in *A House For Biswas,* have an exact parallel in Naipaul's own life. The Character of Mr. Biswas in the novel is modelled on Naipaul's father. Even in his portrayal of the extended family of the Tulsis, Naipaul has drawn considerably from his own experience of having lived in his mother's family house in Chaguanas. The autobiographical element serves to authenticate the East Indians' experience in the West Indies as recorded in the novels, even though it is more an impressionistic record than the literal truth as Naipaul himself makes it clear in his article entitled, "Writing a House for Mr. Biswas."[48] In *House,* all the generations of Indians ranging from indentured labourers like Bipti's father, to the third generation Indians like Savi and Anand find representation.

Naipaul is a much discussed novelist. From the beginning of his literary career he has been surrounded by controversy because of his wry assessment of postcolonial societies. He arouses contrasting responses among his readers who are divided into opposite critical camps. On the one hand there are critics, who pay him endless praise while on the other there are those who, striking the opposite chord, attack him for his unfavourable portrayal of Third World countries in both his fiction as well as non-fiction. The latter are mostly scholars and critics from the Third World, while the former are mostly from the West. Much of the anti-Naipaul criticism comes from the West Indies itself. Surprisingly enough, the response from his Indian critics and scholars has been largely sympathetic in spite of Naipaul's attacks on India, especially in *Area* and *India: A Wounded Civilization.*[49] Here, a brief chronological overview of critical literature on Naipaul would be useful.

With the idea of a separate Commonwealth Literature gaining ground in the 1960s, writers belonging to the ex-colonial English speaking world came into limelight. It was under the aegis of Commonwealth Literature that critical studies on Naipaul first gained ascendancy and made its take off. Contributions poured in from various quarters and the period up to the late eighties witnessed turbulent critical activity.

Paul Theroux, William Walsh, Landeg White, Anthony Boxill and Peter Hughes are some of the prominent names among Naipaul's Western scholars. Some equally eminent names among Third World critics are West Indian critics like George Lamming and Selwyn Cudjoe and Indian critics like C.D. Narasimhaiah, I.K. Madhusudana Rao and Sudha Rai. These critics concentrate mainly on Naipaul's development as a creative artist or the relation between his fiction and non-fiction or on some of the controversial issues relating to Naipaul's portrayal of the Third World.

Paul Theroux, in his book entitled *V.S. Naipaul: An Introduction to His Work*[50] (1972), is mainly interested in the many ideas and themes that repeatedly occur in Naipaul's fiction and non-fiction. After identifying his major themes as "creation," "fantasy," "marriage," "travel" and "freedom," he goes on to discuss the themes, which also form the headings for his chapters. In the last chapter he raises the question of Naipaul's style. William Walsh in his book entitled *V.S. Naipaul*[51] (1973) is mainly interested in the extent and variety of Naipaul's art. Landeg White's book, *V.S. Naipaul: A Critical Introduction*[52] (1975) is a study of Naipaul's development as a writer. He focuses on the ways in which Naipaul's whole career is centred on the uncertainties of his own position and sees the cultural ambiguities of Naipaul's background as the pivot of his works. Anthony Boxill in his book, *V.S. Naipaul's Fiction: In Quest of the Enemy*[53] (1983) identifies a single controlling theme in Naipaul's fiction, which he calls "The Enemy" and argues that through the development of this theme Naipaul makes his human beings more and more responsible for their predicament. Petter Hughes' book, *V.S. Naipaul*[54] (1988) in the series entitled "contemporary writers" concentrates on Naipaul's prose and shows that Naipaul's non-fiction has a "deep and tangled relationship to his fiction."

George Lamming's attack on Naipaul in his book entitled *The Pleasures of Exile*[55] (1960) is only too well-known. It has been discussed in some detail in chapter II. The other West Indian critic Selwyn Cudjoe is equally acerbic in his attack. In his book entitled *V.S. Naipaul: A Materialist Reading*[56] (1988) he tries to show that Naipaul is not politically neutral but writes from the ideological position of the West. Coming to the Indian critics, C.D. Narasimhaiah, the renowned scholar in Commonwealth Literature and editor of collections on Naipaul, is less accommodating in his attitude to Naipaul while K.I. Madhusudana Rao and Sudha Rai adopt a defensive stance towards Naipaul. In his article entitled "V.S. Naipaul: A Split Sensibility,"[57] C.D. Narasimhaiah attacks Naipaul for his lack of sympathy and concern for people in *Area*. In the critic's analysis Naipaul's negative response to India is due to his inability to penetrate the deepest layers of the Indian mind. Madhusudana Rao in his book, *Contrary Awareness: A Critical Study of the Novels of V.S. Naipaul*[58] (1982), closely analyses Naipaul's works and arrives at the positive conclusion that Naipaul's stance is not that of a snob, who is completely bereft of all human sympathy, but that Naipaul works through a "Contrary awareness" which enables him to analyse the deficiencies of ex-colonial societies in a dispassionate manner. Sudha Rai's study *V.S. Naipaul: A Study in Expatriate Sensibility*[59] (1982), focuses on Naipaul's non-fiction. She attempts to assess the merits of Naipaul's judgement on India and argues that because of the complex and confusing amalgam of the "Hindu self" and the "Western self," Naipaul applies the dual cultural norms that his self combines. Thus he measures India by the Hindu norms of *Karma, Dharma* and *Moksha* as well as the Western norms of individuality and freedom. She emphasizes the point that Naipaul's negative judgements do not issue out of indifference or malice and concludes that his judgements on India are perfectly compatible with a deep emotional response to the country.

It was mentioned a few paragraphs earlier that Naipaul criticism up to the eighties was prolific. In the nineties, however critical interest in Naipaul seems to have sagged a bit, probably because Naipaul has become a degree less controversial following his sympathetic stance towards India in *India: A Million mutinies now*[60] (1990) and also more repetitive in his themes. With the emergence of postcolonial Literature, new vistas have opened up for Naipaul scholars. A recent critical volume by Manjit Inder Singh, published in the series entitled "Writers of the Indian Diaspora" is essentially postcolonial in approach. In his book, *V.S. Naipaul*[61] (1998) Manjit Inder Singh working through diaspora and diasporic identification locates Naipaul within the East Indian Caribbean Sub-diaspora abroad. He also concentrates on some of the problematic issues related to the post-colonial critical theory. The present study also adopts the postcolonial approach but differs in focus. It focuses on the problematics of being a postcolonial subject or in other words the repercussions of the colonial encounter on the lives of the colonized as presented in Naipaul's novels.

This study has been undertaken because of the relevance Naipaul's themes bear on the contemporary world. His works throw light on the postcolonial and post-imperial realities that have shaped the contemporary societies and thus provide important insights relating to them. It is hoped that a study of Naipaul's novels may lead to a better understanding of the problems that face the post-imperial generations. In the chapters that follow, we shall examine the themes of the cultural disintegration of the East Indians, mimicry and selfhood as portrayed in the novels of the first phase. In the chapters that deal with the second phase of Naipaul's work we shall focus primarily on the newer themes like the paradoxes of power and freedom in the erstwhile colonies, Naipaul's depiction of the ex-colonies and his vision of the world. However, we shall also touch upon some of those familiar themes of Naipaul, that are reviewed by the novelist consequent to the broadening of his vision.

REFERENCES

1. Ashis Nandy, Preface, *The Intimate Enemy: Loss and Recovery of Self Under Colonialism* (Delhi: Oxford University Press, 1983), xi.
2. Elbaki Hermassi, *The Third World Reassessed* (Berkeley: University of California Press, 1980), 167.
3. Ania Loomba, *Colonialism/Postcolonialism* (London: Routledge, 1998), 3.
4. Jenny Sharpe, "Figures of Colonial Resistance," *Modern Fiction Studies*, 35.1 (1989), 141.
5. John Friedl and John E. Pfeiffer, *Anthropology: The Study of People* (New York: Harper & Row, 1977), 328.
6. Friedl and Pfeiffer, 321.
7. *Ibid.*, 326-27.
8. Nicholas B. Dirks, foreword, *Colonialism and It's Forms of Knowledge: The British in India,* by Bernard S. Cohn (Delhi: Oxford University Press, 1997), ix.

9. Friedl and Pfeiffer, 491.
10. Albert Memmi, *The Colonizer and the Colonized* (London: Earthscan, 1990), 153.
11. Sushanta Goonatilake, *Crippled Minds: An Exploration into Colonial Culture* (New Delhi: Vikas Publishing House, 1982), 129.
12. Edward W. Said, introduction, *Culture and Imperialism*, by Said (London: Vintage, 1994), xiii.
13. Martin Green, *Dreams of Adventure, Deeds of Empire* (London: Routledge and Kegan Paul, 1979), 3.
14. Louis, L. Snyder, ed. *The Imperialism Reader: Documents and Readings on Modern Imperialism* (New York: D Van Nostrand Company, 1962), 87.
15. Elleke Boehmer, *Colonial and Post-colonial Literature*: Migrant Metaphors (New York: Oxford University Press, 1995), 20.
16. Bill Ashcroft, Gareth Griffiths and Helen Tiffin, ed. *The Post Colonial Studies Reader* (London: Routledge, 1995), 284.
17. Elleke Boehmer, 20.
18. Bruce King, Introduction, *West Indian Literature*, ed. King (London: Macmillan, 1979), 6-7.
19. V.S. Naipaul, *The Overcrowded Barracoon* (Harmondsworth: Penguin, 1976), 27.
20. Naipaul, *A House for Mr. Biswas* (Harmondsworth: Penguin, 1969).
21. Naipaul, *The Middle Passage* (Harmondsworth: Penguin, 1969).
22. Naipaul, *The Mimic Men* (Harmondsworth: Penguin, 1969).
23. Naipaul, *Guerrillas* (London: Andre Deutsch, 1975).
24. Naipaul, *A Bend in the River* (Harmondsworth: Penguin, 1980).
25. Naipaul, *A Flag on the Island* (Harmondsworth: Penguin, 1969).
26. Naipaul, *In a Free State* (London: Andre Deutsch, 1971).
27. Naipaul, "People are Proud of Being Stupid," *Newsweek*, 18 Aug. 1980: 38.
28. Naipaul, *Passage*, 43.
29. *Ibid.*, 45.
30. *Ibid.*, 152-53.
31. *Ibid.*, 45.
32. *Ibid.*, 71.
33. *Ibid.*, 71.
34. Eric Williams, *History of the People of Trinidad and Tobago* (London: Andre Deutsch, 1964), 37.
35. Eric Williams, *Trinidad and Tobago*, 211-12.
36. Naipaul, *Passage*, 88.
37. Naipaul, *Finding the Centre* (Harmondsworth: Penguin, 1985).

38. Naipaul, *Centre*, 49.
39. Gerald Moore, "East Indians and West," *Black orpheus* 7 June (1960): 11.
40. Naipaul, *The Mystic Masseur* (Harmondsworth: Penguin, 1964).
41. Naipaul, *The Suffrage of Elvira* (Harmondsworth: Penguin, 1969).
42. Naipaul, *Miguel Street* (London: Andre Deutsch, 1959).
43. Naipaul, *A House for Mr. Biswas* (Harmondsworth: Penguin, 1969).
44. Naipaul, *The Overcrowded Barracoon* (Harmondsworth: Penguin, 1976).
45. Naipaul, *Barracoon*, 38.
46. Naipaul, *An Area of Darkness* (New Delhi: Penguin, 1968).
47. Naipaul, *Area*, 36.
48. Naipaul, "Writing A House for Mr. Biswas," *New York Review of Books*, 24 Nov. 1983, 22.
49. Naipaul, *India: A Wounded Civilization*, (New Delhi: Penguin, 1979).
50. Paul Theroux, *V.S. Naipaul: An Introduction to His Work* (London: Andre Deutsch, 1972).
51. William Walsh, *V.S. Naipaul, The Modern Writers' Series* (Edinburgh: Oliver and Boyd, 1973).
52. Landeg White, *V.S. Naipaul: A Critical Introduction* (London: Macmillan, 1975).
53. Anthony Boxill, *V.S. Naipaul's Fiction: In Quest of the Enemy* (Canada: York Press, 1983).
54. Petter Hughes, *V.S. Naipaul*, Contemporary Writers (London and New York: Routledge, 1988).
55. George Lamming, *The Pleasures of Exile* (London: Michael Joseph, 1960).
56. Selwyn Cudjoe, *V.S. Naipaul: A Materialist Reading* (Amherst: University of Massachusetts Press, 1988).
57. C.D. Narasimhaiah, *The Critical Indian Scene: Controversial Essays* (Delhi: B.R. Publishing Corporation, 1990), 96-109.
58. K.I. Madhusudana Rao, *Contrary Awareness: A Critical Study of the Novels of V.S. Naipaul* (Guntur: Saradhi, 1982).
59. Sudha Rai, *V.S. Naipaul: A Study in Expatriate Sensibility* (New Delhi: Arnold Heinemann, 1982).
60. Naipaul, *India: A Million Mutinies Now* (London: Minerva, 1990).
61. Manjit Inder Singh, *V.S. Naipaul*, Writers of Indian Diaspora (Jaipur: Rawat Publications, 1998).

2

THE PORTRAYAL OF THE CULTURAL DISINTEGRATION OF THE EAST INDIANS IN *THE MYSTIC MASSEUR* AND *THE SUFFRAGE OF ELVIRA*

> Every colonized people—in other words, every people in whose soul an inferiority complex has been created by the death and burial of its local cultural originality—finds itself face to face with the language of the civilizing nation, that is, with the culture of the mother country. The colonized is elevated above his jungle status in proportion to his adoption of the mother country's cultural standards.[1]
>
> —*Frantz Fanon*

The Mystic Masseur, published in 1957, is placed, entirely within the East Indian community and the narrator of the novel himself says that the "history of Ganesh is, in a way the history of our times."[2] So Ganesh, the hero of the novel is a representative figure of the East Indians in Trinidad in their move towards city life and their subsequent creolization. Recognizing this aspect of the novel, Bruce F. MacDonald observes that the novel is "an allegory of the history of the Hindu community in Trinidad."[3]

Ganesh represents the first generation of East Indians to come under the influence of Western education, which acted as a potent force of cultural colonization. The first generation Indians, in particular, faced an acute identity crisis because while their socializing process had been in the traditional culture, they were at the same time introduced to an entirely different value system in the school. It is the need for education that brings Ganesh to the Creole world of Port of Spain.

Mr. Ramsumair, Ganesh's father, makes special preparations for the day Ganesh is to be enrolled into Queen's Royal College:

> Mr. Ramsumair made a lot of noise about sending his son to the 'town college' and the week before the term began he took Ganesh all over the district, showing him off to friends and acquaintances. He had Ganesh dressed in a Khaki suit and a Khaki toupee and many people said the boy looked like a little Sahib.[4]

Ramsumair accompanies Ganesh, dressed in his traditional Indian attire—dhoti, kurta and cap—and the moment they arrive at Port of Spain, they invite looks of ridicule. Ganesh's first day in college turns out to be a humiliating experience, when the boys in the new college make fun of his awkward dress and country manners. For the first time in his life Ganesh is made aware of his marginal position as an Indian. He feels so ashamed that he even tries to hide his Indian identity: "He was so ashamed of his Indian name that for a while he spread a story that he was really called Gareth."[5]

This episode is only the prelude to Ganesh's final transformation at the end of the novel to G. Ramsay Muir. M.B.E. (Member of British Empire). The subtle process of cultural colonization has already begun with the moment of Ganesh's coming into contact with the colonizing culture. Ganesh spends four years in Queen's Royal College without overcoming his awkwardness. Yet, the four years at the college have influenced him greatly as Ganesh's disagreement with his father on the issue of his marriage evidences. In accordance with the traditional custom among the East Indians, Ganesh's father selects a bride for Ganesh and writes to him telling him that he should return home and get married. By this time Ganesh has successfully completed his term in college. However, Ganesh thinks it is too early for marriage and sends a negative reply. This time Ramsumair writes a strong letter giving Ganesh the ultimatum that "if Ganesh didn't want to get married he must consider himself an orphan."[6] Even this threat does not make Ganesh change his mind. He goes against the traditional custom as well as his father's wish, and instead of returning home gets himself enrolled in the

Government Training College for teachers in Port of Spain. He finally returns home only when he receives a telegram and on arriving at Fourways, he gets the news of his father's death.

The short interlude between Ganesh's disagreement with his father and his return to Fourways is significant because it provides a glimpse of a typical colonial school. At the end of Ganesh's training in the Teacher's Training College, he is sent to a school in the East End of Port of Spain. At the very outset, the headmaster of the school gives Ganesh a brief on the purpose of education:

> Mr. Ramsumair, I don't know what views you have about educating the young, but I want to let you know right away, before we even start, that the purpose of this school is to form, not to inform. Everything is planned.[7]

The narrator of the novel, provides an ironic supplement to the passage when he observes:

> Ganesh gave up trying to teach the boys anything, and was happy enough to note a week-to-week improvement in his Record Book. According to that book, the Remove advanced from Theorem One to Theorem Two in successive weeks, and then moved on unexhausted to Theorem Three.[8]

The passages reproduced from the text also demonstrate Naipaul's own technique as a novelist. While remaining detached himself, he allows the characters to damn themselves, but effectively puts across his ideas through the medium of the narrator within the novel. Ganesh's teaching career comes to an end after a dispute with a colleague and the telegram takes him back to Fourways. From this point onwards, until Ganesh's final move to Port of Spain, the narrative oscillates mainly between Fourways and Fuente Grove, and traces the success story of Ganesh upto his victory in the election, and his first experience as a M.L.C. in the dinner party at Government House. The final chapter reports Ganesh's move to Port of Spain and his rise in position from M.L.C. to M.B.E.

In the section of the novel which covers the period between Ganesh's return to Fourways and his winning the election, the East Indian community comes alive. The East Indian communal life is evident in the way they get together in times of joy and sorrow. When Ganesh arrives at Fourways after receiving the telegram, it is half past eleven in the night, yet the entire village is awake. There are scores of people waiting for Ganesh, ready to console him and participate in his grief. All the arrangements for Ramsumair's funeral is managed by the people, most of whom Ganesh does not even know:

> No one asked him about plans for the cremation. Every thing seemed arranged already and Ganesh was content that it should be so. He allowed Ramlogan to take him away from the house, with its sobs and shrieks and lamentations, its gas lamps, oil lamps, bottle flambeaux, bright lights everywhere except in the small bedroom.[9]

Ganesh's aunt, who is nicknamed as "the Great Belcher," not only organises everything, but also bears the entire expense of the cremation. A constant presence in the novel, she exerts a strong influence on Ganesh and is the first person to convince Ganesh that he has the potentials of the mystic. She tells him: "It have a long time now I studying you, Ganesh. You have the Power all right."[10] When Ganesh does not seem convinced, she continues: "Ganesh you have the power. I could see it in your hands, your eyes, in the shape of your head. Just like your uncle, God bless him. He would be a great man today, if only he did live."[11] She has great organising capabilities and is continually on circuit organising funerals and marriages. She is the principal organiser of Ganesh's marriage, which evokes a great deal of excitement and becomes a community affair. Dozens of women, most of whom Ganesh has never seen before, arrive with their children well before the marriage, to keep Ganesh company and take care of the marriage rituals. However, even as we get the feel of the community life of the East Indians, we are at once made aware that the inner bastions of the East Indian culture have begun to fall. This section of the novel also focuses on the role played by the Second World War in bringing about the disintegration of the East Indian community. The cultural upheaval already set in motion by the colonial education system, gained momentum through the modernizing forces unleashed by the Second World War. The economic boom precipitated by the American presence in Trinidad, together with rapid urbanization acted as potent forces of disintegration. In *Barracoon*, Naipaul writes that the East Indians in Trinidad could maintain their cultural insularity only because Trinidad was a "stagnant" society in the nineteenth century. The India that the East Indians had managed to re-create and preserve in Trinidad was an India in Isolation. However, the insularity of the East Indians was broken during the Second World War: "At the first blast from the New World—the Second World War, the coming of Americans to the islands—India fell away, and a new people seemed all at once to have been created."[12] H.S. Mann, a critic discussing the effects of the Second World War on Trinidad, also notes:

> Ill-prepared for the changes thrust on them by World War Two with its economic boom and by universal adult franchise in 1946, Trinidadians turned to trickery, and to the imitation of England and America.[13]

In the later part of the novel, we witness the changes ushered in by the Second World War. It is significant that Ganesh's first success, which is the outcome of the combination of his Western education and Eastern sensibility, gets a boost during the Second World War. Ganesh gets a temple constructed in Fuente Grove and gives it enough publicity to attract the attentions of the American soldiers. Ganesh makes good business when the Americans start pouring into Fuente Grove to see his temple and even seek his spiritual advice.

Naipaul also brings to the fore the inherent dichotomy in the lives of the East Indians in Trinidad. In *Passage*, Naipaul makes the observation that the religion of the East Indians has been reduced to "rites without philosophy."[14] This becomes evident both during Ganesh's initiation ceremony as well as during his marriage. When Ganesh comes home for the first holidays after his admission into Queens Royal College, his father decides that it is time for Ganesh to become a real Brahmin, for which a Hindu should undergo the initiation ceremony. Following the traditional custom, Ganesh's head is shaved, he is given a little saffron bundle and asked to go to Benares to study. As directed, Ganesh begins to walk away from Fourways. In keeping with the custom, Dookhie, the Shopkeeper, runs after Ganesh and begs him not to go away to Benares. The person undergoing initiation is expected to give in to the plea and turn back his steps. Ganesh, however, keeps on walking away making all the people present cry out in bewilderment: "But what happen to the boy?" "He taking this thing really serious."[15] Dookhie too bursts out in anger:

> Cut out this nonsense, man. Stop behaving stupid. You think I have all day to run after you? You think you really going to Benares? That is in India, you know, and this is Trinidad.[16]

Both reactions make it clear that the East Indians are under no delusions. They are well aware of the limitations of the make-believe world they have created for themselves.

The dichotomy is further exemplified during Ganesh's marriage. In a traditional Hindu marriage, the groom is not supposed to have seen his bride before marriage. However, Ganesh and Leela have already met each other. So Ramlogan, Leela's father, and Ganesh have to pretend that Ganesh has never seen Leela because, as the narrator says, "they were both good Hindus and knew it was wrong for a man to see his wife before marriage."[17] The narrator's account makes it clear that the East Indians realize that a strict adherence to traditional customs is no longer possible for them. Yet they cling on to them because of the sentimental value attached to them. In Trinidad they can no longer be good Hindus, they can only act like good Hindus.

The Trinidad Indians also exhibit a tendency typical among people who are victims of what Sushanta Goonatilake calls "Cultural schizophrenia"[18] or the tendency among the colonized, to legitimise their actions in either cultural frames to suit the demands of the situation. Ramlogan tries to avoid the traditional kedgeree-eating ceremony during Ganesh's marriage in order to escape from having to pay Ganesh a dowry. He tells Ganesh:

> Is the shame, sahib, that eating me up. You know how with these Hindu weddings everybody does know how much the boy get from the girl father. When, the morning after the wedding the boy sit down and they give a plate of kedgeree, with the girl father having to give money and keep on giving until the boy eat kedgeree, everybody go see what I give you, and they go say, "Look, Ramlogan

> marrying off his second and best daughter to a boy with a college education, and this is all the man giving." Is that what eating me up, sahib. I know that for you, educated and reading books night and day, it wouldn't mean much, but for me, sahib, what about my character and sensa values?[19]

Ganesh reassures Ramlogan that he would not put him into trouble, but would take only a nominal amount, just for the sake of the custom. Ramlogan then denounces the dowry system in the following words: "Yes, Sahib, the custom. But still I think is a disgrace in these modern times. Now, if I was getting married, I wouldn't want any dowry and I would a say, "To hell with the kedgeree, man."[20] Yet, the same Ramlogan had a little earlier denounced education as an evil: "Education, Sahib, is one hell of a thing. When you is a poor illiterate man like me, all sorts of people, does want to take advantage on you."[21] However, we know that it is only one of Ramlogan's ploys to avoid paying Ganesh a dowry.

In every sphere of the lives of the East Indians—their dress, language and food habits—their cultural confusion becomes apparent. We first witness the confusion through the boy narrator's eyes in the opening chapter itself. When the boy narrator is taken to Ganesh to get his leg cured, Ganesh is still a struggling masseur and the first thing the narrator notices about Ganesh is his dress: "He was dressed in the ordinary way, trousers and vest, and I didn't think he looked particularly holy. He wasn't wearing the dhoti and *koortah* and turban I had expected."[22] There is a contradiction in the fact that while Ganesh follows the traditional profession of a masseur he dons Western clothes. It is only later, on Beharry and Suruj mooma's advice that Ganesh takes to wearing the traditional Indian attire. This is how the couple convince Ganesh:

> 'Yes Ganesh. Me and Suruj Poopa been thinking a lot about you. We thinking that you must stop wearing trousers and a shirt.'
>
> 'It don't suit a mystic,' Beharry said.
>
> 'You must wear proper dhoti and koortah. I was talking

> only last night to Leela about it when she come here to buy cooking-oil. She think is a good idea too.'[23]

Even after Ganesh starts wearing the traditional dress, he does not totally give up the use of Western clothes. For instance, he wears trousers and vest when he goes to meet his friend at the oilfields and feels more confident in them: "He went to Port of Spain—his courage failed him at the last moment and he wore English clothes—to the Registrar-General's Office in the Red House."[24] Towards the end of the novel after Ganesh shifts to Port of Spain, he discards the traditional attire and finally opts for modern Western clothes.

The duality in the lives of the East Indians is clearly evident in their use of language as well. Most of the time they use a dialectal version of English, characterized by the use of misconjugated verbs. Even Ganesh, in spite of his education, uses standard English on rare occasions and is extremely self-conscious while doing so. On one occasion for instance, he tries to speak in formal English with Leela and the episode serves as a good piece of comedy:

> One day he said, 'Leela, is high time we realize that we living in a British country and I think we shouldn't be shame to talk the people language good.'
>
> Leela was squatting at the kitchen *chulha*, coaxing a fire from dry mango twigs. Her eyes were red and watery from the smoke.
>
> 'All right, man.'
>
> 'We starting now self, girl.'
>
> 'As you say, man.'
>
> 'Good. Let me see now. Ah, yes. Leela, have you lighted the fire? No, just gimme a chance. Is "lighted" or "lit," girl?'
>
> 'Look, ease me up, man. The smoke going in my eye.'
>
> 'You ain't paying attention, girl. You mean the smoke is going in your eye.'
>
> Leela coughed in the smoke. 'Look, man. I have a lot more to do than sit scratching, you hear. Go talk to Beharry.'[25]

The passage reflects on the quality of education provided in colonial schools, which have not even been able to teach the correct use of language. We observe that the East Indians hardly use Hindi, which is almost a forgotten language. The only person we hear using the language is Ganesh's father, who dies even before the novel has really begun. So completely has English replaced Hindi, that it has taken its place even in the rituals that the East Indians have managed to preserve. Dookhie, uses English, instead of Hindi when he performs his part in Ganesh's initiation ceremony: "As arranged, Dookhie the shopkeeper ran after him [Ganesh] crying a little and begging in English, 'No, boy. No. Don't go away to Benares to study."[26] The East Indians themselves are unable to see the contradiction because the process of cultural colonization has worked on them unconsciously.

In the case of food habits, we find that the staple is still rice or *roti* and *dal* and a certain fastidiousness about food, which is typically Hindu, still survives. Yet, the Western alternatives have also been adopted. Ganesh's Hindu instincts rise and he feels nauseated to bite into the cold egg-and-cress sandwich, which Mr. Stewart offers him. However, the same Ganesh, has no such hesitations when Ramlogan offers him fish with bread and butter.

The source of Ganesh's cultural ambiguity is undoubtedly, the conflict between the Eastern and Western worlds in which Ganesh finds himself trapped. We see that Ganesh while being attracted, on the one hand, to Western books—he buys many books and even writes books himself—is at the same time inclined to take up massaging. Significantly, his first booklet, *101 Questions and Answers on the Hindu Religion*, turns out to be a "catechism" on the Hindu religion and serves to underline Ganesh's cultural mix. When the booklet does not sell, Ganesh decides to become a masseur. He is successful only after he has learnt to combine the merits of both worlds, Eastern spiritualism and Western learning, to effect the cure of Hector, the boy tormented by a cloud. This characteristic sets Ganesh apart from the hundreds in the same profession. As the narrator points out: "His prestige was secured by his learning. Without this he might easily have been lumped with the other thaumaturges who swarmed over Trinidad. They were nearly all fakes."[27]

Apart from his Western learning, his attitude to religion, which can be traced to Hinduism's tolerant stance also ensures his success:

> He was no bigot. He took as much interest in Christianity and Islam as in Hinduism. In the Shrine, the old bedroom, he had pictures of Mary and Jesus next to Krishna and Vishnu; a crescent and star represented iconoclastic Islam. 'All the same God,' he said. Christians liked him, Muslims liked him, and Hindus willing as ever to risk prayers to new gods, didn't object.[28]

The blend of the East and the West in Ganesh makes him "a sharp character." In *Passage*, writing about Trinidad, Naipaul observes:

> Trinidad has always admired the 'Sharp character' who, like the sixteenth-century Picaroon of Spanish literature, survives and triumphs by his wits in a place where it is felt that all eminence is arrived at by crookedness.[29]

It is this aspect of the society of Trinidad that Naipaul has tried to capture in the character of Ganesh. Ganesh is exposed through the subtle narrative strategy adopted by Naipaul. Irony is built into the very structure of the narrative through the mode of narration. The story of Ganesh comes to us through a dual perspective. On the one hand there is Ganesh's own account of his successful career and on the other, there is the boy narrator's perspective which contradicts Ganesh's version. In his autobiography entitled *The Years of Guilt*, Ganesh writes that his marriage to Leela was preordained, a work of fate which he knew and never questioned: "I had always, from the first day I stepped into Shri Ramlogan's shop, considered it as settled that I was going to marry his daughter. I never questioned it. It all seemed Preordained."[30] However, the boy narrator's account of what happened shows that Ganesh accepts the proposal only after Ramlogan has revealed the exact worth of his property:

> 'That is it, sahib. Just just as you say. Is all Good work. Count my property now. Is true I is illiterate, but you just sit down in that hammock and count my property.'

> Ramlogan was walking with such unusual energy that sweat broke and shone on his forehead. Suddenly he halted and stood directly in front of Ganesh. He took away his hands from behind his back and started to count off his fingers. 'Two acres near Chaguanas. Good land too. Ten acres in penal. You never know when I could scrape together enough to make the drillers put an oil-well there. A house in Fuente Grove. Not much but is something. Two three houses in Siparia. Add up all that and you find you looking at a man worth about twelve thousand dollars, cool cool.'
>
> Ramlogan passed his hand over his forehead and behind his neck. 'I know is hard to believe, sahib. But is the gospel truth. I think is a good idea, sahib, for you to marriage Leela.'
>
> 'All right,' Ganesh said.[31]

Ganesh achieves success by exercising his wit and intelligence and equally through trickery. He tricks Ramlogan, who deliberately tries to avoid giving Ganesh a dowry, and manages to extract a sizeable dowry from him. Yet, Ganesh wins our sympathy because he is not an outright fake. There are some genuine human qualities in him that deserve commendation. His concern for Hector, the boy tormented by a black cloud, is genuine and he prepares diligently to cure him. His generosity is also evident in his treatment of Ramlogan. In spite of the quarrels between them, Ganesh treats Ramlogan hospitably which warms Leela's heart towards him:

> Leela had tears in her eyes. 'Man, is the second time in my life you make me feel proud of you.' She leaned on him.
>
> He didn't push her away.
>
> 'The first time was with the boy and the cloud. Now is with Pa.'[32]

However, as Ganesh's fortune rises, he is forced to make compromises due to circumstances as well as pressures from the people around him, whose fortunes are tied to his own. Beharry we see, prospers only because of Ganesh. He makes a considerable profit through the sale of land when the land values rise in Feunte Grove due to Ganesh's popularity. As for Leela, Ganesh's success brings a remarkable change in her speech, dress and mannerism:

> Everyday Leela became more refined. She often went to San Fernando to visit Soomintra, and to shop. She came back with expensive saris and much heavy jewellery. But the most important change was in her English. She used a private accent which softened all harsh vowel sounds; her grammar owed nothing to anybody, and included a highly personal conjugation of the verb to be.[33]

Leela reacts to Ganesh's success by mimicking upperclass respectability. We are reminded that it is a typical colonial society where people are unsure of themselves and having no taste or style of their own are eager for instruction. In his autobiography Ganesh acknowledges the insignificance of the individual will when he writes: "We are never what we want to be...but what we must be."[34] Egged on by Leela, Beharry and Suruj Mooma, Ganesh is forced to commercialize his profession. He first opens a restaurant and then takes over the taxi business from Ramlogan. Upto this point, however, Ganesh has made no major compromise with his basic integrity. But his fall comes when he becomes the president of the Hindu Association by defeating Narayan, his opponent, in a carefully planned political manoeuvre. From this point onwards Naipaul's satire assumes a sharpness and by the end of the novel all sympathy towards Ganesh is withdrawn.

After becoming the President of the Hindu Association, Ganesh contests the election and fights, as the narrator ironically says, "the cleanest election campaign in Trinidad history."[35] Ganesh, unlike his rival, Indersingh, holds no election meetings. Instead, he cleverly arranges a "Bhagwat"—seven day prayer meeting with free food. Ganesh understands people inside-out, and Indersingh even with the glamour of his Oxford degree stands no chance before Ganesh. After becoming a M.L.C. Ganesh attends a dinner party at the Government House. The dinner party serves as a commentary on the shortcomings of a society striving to mimic upperclass respectability, which at once contradicts their social reality. For instance, among those who attend the party, there is an elderly East Indian

Christian, who comes along with his daughter but has not brought his wife because "he never had one."[36] As Naipaul describes the dinner party, his language takes on an increasingly corrosive tinge:

> The dinner was a treat for the photographers. Ganesh came in *dhoti* and *koortah* and turban; the member for one of the Port of Spain wards wore a khaki suit and a sun helmet; a third came in jodhpurs; a fourth, adhering for the moment to his pre-election principles, came in short trousers and an open shirt; the blackest M.L.C. wore a three-piece blue suit, yellow woolen gloves and a monocle. Everybody else, among, the men, looked like penguins, sometimes even down to the black faces.[37]

Ganesh's experience at the dinner is a torturous one. He is left feeling "alien and uncomfortable,"[38] throughout the party. Incidentally, this happens to be the last time Ganesh appears in traditional clothes. Soon after the dinner episode, Ganesh shifts to Port of Spain, where he stops wearing dhoti and turban altogether. As a M.L.C., he frequently stages walkouts and though he becomes the most popular man in Trinidad because he never charges high fees for the favours he bestows, he has not yet come into the notice of the colonial office, which in its reports dismisses him as "an irresponsible agitator."[39] However, when Ganesh, unable to quell the strike in the sugar estates, pins the blame on the communists and also declares his determination to fight against them, the colonial office begins to take notice of him. Its reports now describe Ganesh as "an important political leader."[40] Soon, he is made the representative of the British Government and sent to Lake Success, where Ganesh speaks in defence of British colonial rule and this finally fetches him the title of M.B.E.

By this time Ganesh has travelled far on the road to whiteness, but his final rejection of his society comes with his change of name to G. Ramsay Muir. What finally damns him in the eyes of the readers is the complete change in his manners, which is reflected in his cold and formal response to the narrator's warm and friendly greeting. Ganesh's transformation to a capitalist and mimic man is now complete.

Naipaul draws attention to the inadequacies of colonial societies which are often characterised by a lack of acumen for specialization. Trinidad is portrayed as a society in upheaval, where the old order is giving way to new forces of modernity and the East Indian community of which Ganesh is a representative is particularly vulnerable. Ganesh's success story is really the story of the disintegration of the East Indian community, which under the conflicting pull of the Eastern and Western worlds, makes the final choice in favour of the Western civilization.

Masseur has elicited a lot of critical response. Much of the criticism directed against it is related to the structure of the novel. The review of the novel in the "Times Literary Supplement" reads: "Naipaul's strength seems to be in the presentation of individual episodes and scenes, and not to be entirely equal to the strains of a full-length novel" (qtd. in Landeg White: 74). Landeg White also discerns strains in the ending of the novel. The criticism is not unfounded. The final chapter gives an impression of being cramped. Many incidents crucial to the understanding of the novel, an elaboration of which would certainly have enhanced the reader's perception of the novel, are vaguely presented.

Besides the structural shortcomings, Naipaul has been severely criticised for his treatment of the colonial people which is felt to be lacking in sympathy. The dinner scene has been particularly targeted. Commenting on the scene, Gordon Rohlehr makes the following observation:

> One can accept this as farce intended, in its distorted way, to show the Creole and Indian on the painful and ridiculous road to whiteness. But the suspicion persists that Naipaul himself regards these people; with more contempt than compassion.[41]

A similar observation is made by A.C. Derrick in his article entitled "Naipaul's techniques as a Novelist": "The cold detachment with which he can present human shortcomings is a measure of the brutality of his wit and at times makes reading his work rather like a clinical exercise."[42]

On the other hand, Landeg White, while agreeing that the dinner scene is "unnecessarily cruel," considers it more relevant to focus on the "balancing moments" in the novel in which Naipaul gives an extremely sensitive portrayal of the contradictions in which the characters are trapped.[43] As Rohlehr points out: "Satire is the sensitive measure of a society's departure from a norm inherent in itself."[44] Rohlehr also perceives that Naipaul's task as a satirist was, "doubly difficult," as he started with the conviction that such a norm was absent from his society. He had to re-create experience and simultaneously create the standards against which the experience was to be judged.[45] Naipaul may seem cruel and unsympathetic but it is only because he is annoyed by the West Indians' appropriation of Western cultural norms, which clearly cannot be their's.

While *Masseur* focuses on the rural society of the East Indians, Naipaul's next novel, *Suffrage*, completes the picture by examining the political dimensions of the society, where democracy is a newly-born concept. It was written, as Naipaul himself says, "to prove to myself that I could invent a story around a given incident."[46] Clearly, Naipaul wanted to meet the challenge thrown open to him by the book review of *Masseur*.

Suffrage is constructed around a single event the second general elections in Elvira. Set during the second general elections, the novel examines the East Indian community within the context of the newly emerging colonial-capitalist society during a period of growing social and political awareness. There are definite references in *Suffrage* to characters and events which make it clear that the novel is a continuation of *Masseur*. In chapter six there is a specific reference to Ganesh. After Herbert's spiritual fumigation, Baksh says:

> Ganesh Pundit was really the man for this sort of mystic thing. Pity he had to take up politics. Still that show how good he was. The moment he feel he was losing his hand for that sort of thing, he give up the business.[47]

Ramlogan also reappears in *Suffrage* as the owner of a rumshop. That he is the same Ramlogan is confirmed from what Chittaranjan says about him in the second chapter: "For three years now, since the man come to live in Elvira, he only giving me provocation."[48] In addition, there is a reference to the first general elections of nineteen forty-six which was the major event in the preceding novel. The *Suffrage* then, picks up the strands of the story at the point where *Masseur* had left off. At the end of *Masseur,* the East Indian community had come into contact with the Creole world of Port of Spain. Suffrage opens up into the broader social context of multiracial Elvira and includes the Negro and Spanish population as well.

The thrust of the novel is to demonstrate how unsuitable the modern concept of democracy is for a corrupt and divided colonial society, in which democracy loses all meaning and becomes a means for promoting self-interest. In *Passage,* Naipaul observes that universal adult suffrage came to Trinidad in nineteen forty-six, without any popular agitation, taking the people by surprise. People were unprepared for it and only "the enterprising, who had seen the prodigious commercial possibilities,"[49] had been able to make the most of it. By the second general elections, however, people had become aware of the value of their votes, and were out to exploit the candidates. In *Suffrage,* when Harbans, the Hindu candidate, tells Baksh, the Muslim vote bank that in the nineteen forty-six elections none of the candidates he knew had spent as much as he was having to, Baksh immediately replies: "But that was only the fust election. People did just go and vote for the man they like. Now is different. People learning. You have to spend on them."[50]

Everyone is out to take bribes. Elvira is an Indian dominated area, yet for Pat Harbans, the Hindu candidate, this in itself is not assurance enough for victory. The votes may as well go to the Negro candidate Preacher, because one "owed no loyalty to the island, and scarcely any to his group."[51] Under the circumstances only philistine values dominate and determine which candidate would win the elections. The disintegration of the East Indians is evidenced in their opportunism. Harichand, the printer, blackmails Harbans: "If you want my vote, you want my printery."[52]

In *Suffrage,* Naipaul reveals both the candidates as well as the electorate as tricksters. Harbans is prepared to give any bribe in exchange for votes. He concedes to Baksh's demands even though it far exceeds what was initially agreed upon. He even goes to the extent of trading a marriage alliance with Chittaranjan, who is not only the Hindu leader but also "the only man who carried weight with the Spaniards of Cordoba."[53] Harbans wants the votes and Chittaranjan wants his daughter Nelly married to Harbans's son and the bargain is implicitly settled between them. "Lakshmi" was always the patron Goddess, but now under the influence of capitalism people have turned into worshippers of Mammon. This is evident in the second chapter when the reason for Chittaranjan's importance is provided: "Easily the most important person in Elvira was Chittaranjan. And there was no mystery why. He looked rich and was rich."[54]

The Elvirans' propensity for money is revealed in their priorities. Money is placed topmost, even above religion. Baksh, the other power of Elvira, becomes the Muslim leader because he is a man of reputed wealth, even though he is not a good Muslim:

> It was a puzzle: how Baksh came to be the Muslim leader. He wasn't a good Muslim. He didn't know all the injunction of the Prophet and those he did know he broke. For instance he was a great drinker.[55]

While in *Masseur*, only the leader resorted to trickery, now each and every one has turned deceitful. The confused moral values is evidenced in little Herbert's claim that the top is his because he stole it from his school mate: "Is my top. I thief it from a boy at school. Big Lambie."[56]

The tone of ironic detachment as well as the third person omniscient point of view that Naipaul adopts, serve to expose the vices of the society and secure the reader's censure. *Suffrage* marks an important stage in the development of Naipaul as a novelist. While the novels preceding *Suffrage* (*Street* was Naipaul's first work though it was published third) were episodic and loose knit, *Suffrage* is a sustained piece of narrative. His skill as a novelist surfaces in passages where Naipaul subtly exposes the vices of the society and at once directs the reader's response. In the following passage we are given an insight into the nature of the election in Elvira:

> He [Harbans] had done all his bargaining for the elections; the political correspondents said he had as good as won

> already. This afternoon he was going to offer himself formally to Baksh and Chittaranjan, the powers of Elvira. The bargains had only to be formally sealed.[57]

The presentation of characters in *Suffrage* is such that none of the Characters, except perhaps Foam, elicit a sympathetic response from the readers. In a world governed by selfish interests Foam, Baksh's eldest son and Harbans's campaign manager is the most humane of the lot. Foam too, has a personal reason for supporting Harbans. He works "not so much for the victory of Harbans and the defeat of Preacher, as for the humiliation of Lorkhoor and Teacher Francis."[58] Yet, he wins the reader's sympathy because he has one redeeming feature—his loyalty to Harbans till the end. When his father decides to withdraw his support to Harbans after his quarrel with Chittaranjan, Foam tells his father decisively: "Well, I take Harbans money and I give him my word. I going to still help Harbans."[59]

Though everyone is out to extract bribes, Baksh surpasses all in this general propensity. He is the most deceitful of the lot and remains a veritable troublemaker till the end. Even after extracting a double bribe from Harbans he is not satisfied and threatens to support Preacher, the Negro candidate, and even go up for the elections himself. Chittaranjan, who is equally shrewd sees an advantage in this too. He tells Harbans that they should encourage Baksh to contest the elections. He explains to Harbans: "Once the Muslims don't vote for Preacher, we all right."[60] His intention is to split the votes of the opposition. When Harbans goes to talk to Baksh about it he discovers that it is just another of Baksh's ploys to extract a bribe. Harbans is forced to pay Baksh two thousand dollars over and above the deposit money to induce Baksh to go up for the elections. Even after that, Baksh does not stop creating trouble for Harbans, but threatens to sell out to Preacher. However, Mr. Cuffy's death frustrates Baksh's intentions and brightens the prospects for Harbans by providing him with an opportunity to ensure the Negro votes. Harbans arranges for Cuffy's funeral in a big way in order to win the Negro votes by generating their sympathy in his favour. There is utter confusion just before the elections with everybody selling out to somebody. In fact as Foam points out: "In Trinidad you can't say anybody win election till they draw their first pay."[61]

Finally, it is Harbans who wins the elections but it leaves a bitter taste in his mouth. His brand new jaguar is set on fire in the final scene when Harbans comes to Elvira for the first time after becoming a Member of Legislative Council to give away the case of whisky, which Ramlogan had promised the committee of the winning candidate. Yet Harbans himself is in a way responsible for what happens as the passage shows:

> He wasn't the candidate they knew. Gone was the informality of dress, the loose trousers, the tie around the waist, the open shirt. He was in a double-breasted grey suit...Harbans didn't wave. He looked preoccupied, kept his eye on the ground, and when he hawked and spat in the gutter, pulled out an ironed handkerchief and wiped his lips—not wiped even, patted them—in the fussiest way.
>
> The people of Elvira were hurt.[62]

Harbans's transformation into a typical politician is complete at the end of the novel when he goes back on his promise to Chittaranjan on the pretext of the false scandal involving Nelly and Foam. When Chittaranjan visits Harbans in Port of Spain, the latter acts busy, remains tight-lipped and coolly tells Harbans: "we cannot let our children marry people who does run about late at night with muslim boys."[63]

The acculturation of the East Indians is a major theme in the early novels of Naipaul and though *Suffrage* focuses on a political event, it does so only to expose the social tensions of a racially divided society like Trinidad. The cultural confusion and the breakdown of religious values are aptly described in passages like the following:

> Things were crazily mixed up in Elvira. Everybody, Hindus, Muslims and Christians, owned a Bible; the Hindus and Muslims looking on it, if anything, with greater awe. Hindus and Muslims celebrated Christmas and Easter. The Spaniards and some of the Negroes celebrated the Hindu festival of lights. Someone had told them that Lakshmi, the Goddess of prosperity, was being honoured; they placed small earthen lamps on their money-boxes

> and waited, as they said, for the money to breed. Everybody celebrated the Muslim festival of Hosein. In fact, when Elvira was done with religious festivals, there were few straight days left.[64]

The impression of amity that the passage seems to offer turns out to be an illusion, when the election brings to surface all sorts of prejudices. Feelings of religious and racial hatred flare up between Chittaranjan and Baksh because of the false scandal involving their children, Nelly and Foam. The insults they aim at each other expose the race relations in Elvira: "What is Muslim?" Chittaranjan asked, his smile frozen, his eyes unshining, his voice low and cutting. 'Muslim is everything and Muslim is nothing.' He paused, 'Even Negro is Muslim.'[65] Basksh's retort is equally venomous: "All you is just a pack of Kaffir, if you ask me."[66]

The cultural confusion of the East Indians portrayed in *Suffrage* is clearly evident in their clothing, which is more pronouncedly Western. Mrs. Baksh wears skirts instead of the traditional Indian attire. Harbans and Chittaranjan wear trousers and shirt. Even pundit Dhaniram, the best known pundit in Elvira, wears a dhoti only occasionally. In his "other more substantial role as the owner of one-fifth of a tractor,"[67] he wears "khaki trousers, yellow sports shirt, brown felt hat and brown patent leather shoes."[68] It is interesting to note that pundit Dhaniram is educated at a Presbyterian school and sings hymns as well. He is even proud of his training in the Christian school because as he says, it makes him "see both sides."[69] As far as the use of language is concerned, we note that the East Indians of multi-racial Elvira are as out of touch with Hindi as the East Indians portrayed in *Masseur*. Except for Dhaniram's invalid wife, no one else speaks the language.

In a society dominated by materialistic values, it is inevitable that conventional customs should also yield to political interests. While in a conventional Hindu marriage, it is the girl's father, who is expected to humbly approach the boy's father for an alliance, in *Suffrage* however, we see quite the opposite happening. Harbans wants the votes controlled by Chittaranjan and so it is he who has to be solicitous. The influence of politics on the behaviour patterns of the people is seen in the way even traditions are compromised for the sake of political advancement. The breakdown of the Hindu social order is also suggested through incidents like Dhaniram's daughter-in-law's elopement with Lorkhoor. We are told that Dhaniram's son had deserted her only two months after marriage and no one knows where he had gone.

While portraying the disintegration of the East Indians, Naipaul provides us a close view of the society. The pervasive influence of social beliefs on political mores in Trinidad is beautifully highlighted by Naipaul. The society of Elvira is traditionally superstitious and so politics also comes to be governed by Obeah and black magic. Tiger, a colicky puppy that Foam and Herbert bring home, out of pity is feared to be an obeah dog and becomes a terror for the Elvirans. Everything is interpreted in superstitious terms. For instance, Foam as Harban's campaign manager daubs the slogan "VOTE HARBANS OR DIE," in the Spanish locality of Cordoba. Lorkhoor, Preacher's campaign manager tries to erase the slogans by covering them up with white-wash. However, the slogans get only partially wiped out. In one particular spot the letters that remain visible can be read as "TEN DIE." This is enough to spread another wave of terror among the people, who take it as a sign portending evil. It is made clear that in a corrupt society even democracy, which equalizes people cannot work. As Teacher Francis in the novel realizes, universal suffrage has done more harm than good: "Elvira was a good friendly place before this Universal Suffrage nonsense."[70]

What makes *Suffrage* different from the other novels in the grouping is the inclusion of Negro characters. There are four in all: Preacher, Cuffy, Sebastian and Teacher Francis. One must admit that Naipaul's handling of these characters lacks the deftness he shows in the delineation of the East Indian characters. Preacher's role as one of the candidates is a substantial one, but his characterization borders on the grotesque. His physical description makes him appear weird:

> A tall Negro with high frizzy hair, long frizzy beard, long white robe; haloed in the light of the headlamps; walking briskly at the edge of the road, stamping his staff, the hem of his robe dancing above sandalled feet.[71]

His reappearance after a long interval with a large stone in his hand and again with a Bible in his right hand and the same stone in his left hand, projects him in a ludicrous light. His major function in the novel is to pose a threat to Harbans.

Sebastian is just a minor character who hardly speaks. Nevertheless, his presence lends a comic touch to the novel. The scenes in which Mahadeo, Harbans's party member, shows obsessive concern for Sebastian are truly comic. Mr. Cuffy, in spite of being a more substantial character compared to Preacher and Sebastian, somehow appears insipid. He is dull as a living character but his death, over which a lot of fuss is made by Harbans and his party members for the sake of publicity, creates a sensation. The more convincing of all the Negro characters presented in the novel is Teacher Francis. Though he plays no major role and is not directly involved in the election, he manages to create an impression on the minds of the readers, probably because he is made accessible to us in a way that the others are not. He is, as Landeg White points out, "the only character who views events with an intelligent detachment,"[72] and provides insightful comments about the elections. Naipaul however, disposes off this character quite suddenly halfway through the novel. We learn at the end that he "deteriorated rapidly"[73] in Port of Spain.

On the whole, Naipaul seems uncomfortable handling the Negro characters and does not display the same dexterity as he does in his portrayal of the East Indian characters. The reason, though, is not far to seek. Naipaul's upbringing was in the enclosed Indian community with hardly any contact with the Negro world. As he observes in *Area* the Indian and Negro worlds were "juxtaposed and mutually exclusive."[74] It is clear that Naipaul did not have access to the kind of understanding required to portray Negro characters with a greater depth.

Critical responses to the novel vary from commendation to bitter condemnation. Landeg White appreciates the novel for its tightly knit story but also points out that this has been achieved by resorting to "a good deal of caricature."[75] The most incisive criticism however, comes from Peter Nazareth. "What is astonishing about the novel," says Nazareth, "is that it is a sustained exercise in contempt for people. There is no person in this novel for whom there is sympathy or understanding."[76] One cannot agree with the critic that the novel is a "sustained exercise in contempt for people." Had Naipaul felt only contempt for people, characters like Foam and Herbert would never have found a place in the novel. Foam's loyalty to Harbans and Herbert's tenderness towards the puppy are noble qualities that Naipaul recognizes. The idea he seeks to put across is that though noble human qualities are as much present in Trinidad, as anywhere else, they cannot flower in the stultifying colonial environment of Trinidad.

Initially, Naipaul did not find a favourable response in the intellectual circles of the West Indies. George Lamming, a fellow West Indian novelist, who came out with a bitter criticism while assessing these novels has this to say:

> His books can't move beyond a castrated satire; and although satire may be a useful element in fiction, no important work, comparable to Selvon's can rest safely on satire alone. When such a writer is a colonial, ashamed of his cultural background and striving like mad to prove himself through promotion to the peaks of a 'superior' culture whose values are gravely in doubt, then satire, like the charge of philistinism, is for me nothing more than a refuge. And it is too small a refuge for a writer who wishes to be taken seriously.[77]

Lamming's attack draws attention to the fundamental literary problem faced by writers who apply the assumptions and resources of English Literature to non-European societies.[78] Naipaul himself acknowledges the problem when he says:

> All the novels I had read were about settled and organised societies and I was aware of a slight fraudulence in applying a form created by that society to the squalor, disorder and shallowness of my own (qtd. in Hayman 58).

Though Lamming's attack appears to be motivated by personal reasons, yet it cannot be dismissed as entirely baseless. There is an element of truth, at least in so far as the ending of *Suffrage* is concerned. It has been pointed out that the weakest part of Naipaul's novels are the endings. While for the most part his irony is tinged with good humour and understanding there are moments when his satire assumes a sharpness. One such instance is evident towards the end of *Suffrage* when Harban's car is set on fire by the Elvirans and he cries out in disgust and hatred: "Elvira, you is a bitch,"[79] and leaves Elvira for good. It is perhaps, the note of rejection on which the novels end that is unacceptable to Lamming, who believes that novels which expose the inadequacies of underprivileged societies like the West Indies, should employ a sympathetic approach.

However, Naipaul is not an irresponsible ironist as some critics think. On the contrary it is his commitment to truth as well as his belief in the novel as a form a social enquiry that makes him reveal the shortcomings of his society as well as other colonial societies. Moreover, Naipaul's subsequent novels *House* and *Mr. Stone and the Knights' Companion*,[80] have made Lamming's accusations seem very much out of target. In *House*, Naipaul's sensitive and sympathetic presentation of Biswas's character nullifies Lamming's criticism that his books cannot move beyond a castrated satire. In *Mr. Stone* on the other hand, Naipaul explodes the myth that England is the Centre of life by exposing the drabness of English life as well.

In *Passage*, Naipaul clarifies his position as a writer. At the same time he laments the fact that West Indian writers have failed in their responsibility towards their society:

> Living in a borrowed culture, the West Indian, more than most, needs writers to tell him who he is and where he stands. Here the West Indian writers have failed. Most have so far only reflected and flattered the prejudices of their race or colour group. Many writers have displayed a concern, visible perhaps only to the West Indian, to show how removed his group is from blackness, how close to whiteness.[81]

It is Naipaul's strong conviction, that in the context of the Caribbean, the use of "irony" and "satire" would help more than the propagandist tendencies adopted by most West Indian writers. He especially emphasizes the point that "blackness" cannot be the basis of any serious literature. Meenakshi

Mukherjee, an important critic of the post-colonial academy agrees on the point when she says:

> The novels written in the Third World which will survive are the ones that go beyond mere political protest and racial anger. These would be seen to encompass issues which are complex—not clear-cut, not black-and-white, expressing a truth which while being rooted in history and geography has the power to transcend these forces.[82]

Though, even in Naipaul's works there is a constant awareness of the slave past of the West Indies, it forms only one of the many strands that inform his larger vision, which is also why he has been able to find a place among writers of the mainstream.

REFERENCES

1. Frantz Fanon, *Black Skin White Masks,* Trans., Charles Lammarkmann (London: Pluto, 1986), 18.
2. Naipaul, *Masseur,* 18.
3. Bruce F. MacDonald, "Symbolic action in Three of V.S. Naipaul's novels," *Critical Perspectives on V.S. Naipaul,* ed. R.D. Hamner (London: Heinemann, 1977), 243.
4. Naipaul, *Masseur,* 19.
5. *Ibid.,* 20.
6. *Ibid.,* 23.
7. *Ibid.,* 24.
8. *Ibid.,* 25.
9. *Ibid.,* 30.
10. *Ibid.,* 116.
11. *Ibid.,* 116.
12. *Ibid.,* 40.
13. H.S. Mann, "Variation on the theme of Mimicry: Naipaul's *The Mystic Masseur* and *The Suffrage of Elivra.*" *Modern Fiction Studies,* 30.3 (1984): 171.
14. Naipaul, *Passage,* 89.
15. Naipaul, *Masseur,* 21.
16. *Ibid.,* 21.
17. *Ibid.,* 48.
18. Sushanta Goonatilake, *Crippled minds,* 130.
19. Naipaul, *Masseur,* 51.
20. *Ibid.,* 51.

21. Naipaul, *Masseur*, 50.
22. *Ibid.*, 13.
23. *Ibid.*, 124.
24. *Ibid.*, 158.
25. *Ibid.*, 76-77.
26. *Ibid.*, 21.
27. *Ibid.*, 138.
28. *Ibid.*, 139.
29. Naipaul, *Passage*, 78.
30. Naipaul, *Masseur*, 46.
31. *Ibid.*, 48.
32. *Ibid.*, 202-03.
33. *Ibid.*, 155.
34. *Ibid.*, 75.
35. *Ibid.*, 199.
36. *Ibid.*, 207.
37. *Ibid.*, 207.
38. *Ibid.*, 209.
39. *Ibid.*, 214.
40. *Ibid.*, 219.
41. Gordon Rohlehr, "The Ironic Approach: The Novels of V.S. Naipaul," *Critical Perspectives*, 181.
42. A.C. Derrick, "Naipaul's Technique as a novelist," *Critical Perspectives*, 194.
43. Landeg White, V.S. Naipaul: *A Critical Introduction*, (London: Macmillan, 1975), 66.
44. Gordon Rohlehr, "The Ironic Approach," *Critical Perspectives*, 179.
45. Rohlehr, "The Ironic Approach," *Critical Perspectives*, 179.
46. Naipaul, "Speaking of Writing," *Times*, 2 Jan. 1964: 11.
47. Naipaul, *Suffrage*, 80.
48. *Ibid.*, 34.
49. Naipaul, *Passage*, 78.
50. Naipaul, *Suffrage*, 46.
51. Naipaul, *Passage*, 78.
52. Naipaul, *Suffrage*, 73.
53. *Ibid.*, 24.
54. *Ibid.*, 24.
55. *Ibid.*, 13.
56. *Ibid.*, 74.
57. *Ibid.*, 12.

58. Naipaul, *Suffrage*, 40.
59. *Ibid.*, 122.
60. *Ibid.*, 143.
61. *Ibid.*, 185.
62. *Ibid.*, 196-97.
63. *Ibid.*, 207.
64. *Ibid.*, 66.
65. *Ibid.*, 114.
66. *Ibid.*, 114.
67. *Ibid.*, 128.
68. *Ibid.*, 128.
69. *Ibid.*, 48.
70. *Ibid.*, 85.
71. *Ibid.*, 37.
72. Landeg White, *V.S. Naipaul: A Critical Introduction*, 85.
73. Naipaul, *Suffrage*, 207.
74. Naipaul, *Area*, 35.
75. Landeg White, *V.S. Naipaul: A Critical Introduction*, 76.
76. Peter Nazareth, "*The Mimic Men* as a study of Corruption," *Critical Perspectives*, 144.
77. George Lamming, *The Pleasures of Exile*, 225.
78. Landeg White, *V.S. Naipaul: A Critical Introduction*, 12.
79. Naipaul, *Suffrage*, 206.
80. Naipaul, *Mr. Stone and the Knights Companion* (London: Penguin, 1973).
81. Naipaul, *Passage*, 73.
82. Meenakshi Mukherjee, "Caliban's Growth: Impact of Colonialism on Commonwealth Fiction," *Colonial Consciousness in Commonwealth Literature*, eds. Amur and Desai (Bombay: Somaiya Publications 1984), 227.

3

Cultural Disintegration and The Search for an Authentic Selfhood in *Miguel Street* and *A House for Mr. Biswas*

"I didn't know who I was"[1]

—*V.S. Naipaul*

In colonial societies, the crisis of identity of the colonized often seems to over-ride all other considerations. In the context of the Caribbean this crisis takes on an even more acute form, for the very basis on which identity anchors itself was completely destroyed by colonization. The social identity of a people is rooted in their culture, while at the individual level, it is determined by personal achievements. In order to experience a "wholeness," it is necessary to fuse the individual and the social consciousness. However, the paradox of the modern predicament lies in the fact that owing to the fragmentation of societies, the affinity that was once felt between the two has now been broken. In the case of artificially created colonial societies like Trinidad, this split becomes even more pronounced.

The history of Trinidad has followed the abnormal, course of conquest, colonization and domination. We know that the indigenous population of Trinidad was virtually decimated during the initial stages of Spanish occupation of Trinidad. Linda A. Newson, in her intensive study on the impact of Spanish colonization on Trinidad, points out that the main cause of the decline in the indigenous population was "the enslaving raids of the Spanish and the Caribs."[2] The decline continued despite the policy of segregation adopted by the Spanish Crown in order to protect the indigenous population.

This was largely due to lack of medical attention during epidemics. The final blow came when the indigenous Indians were integrated into the larger society under the influence of egalitarian doctrines, which were opposed to the idea of segregation.[3] The result was, rapid assimilation of the indigenous population into other communities. The influx of foreign immigrants, following the liberalization of official attitudes towards immigration, completely altered the social makeup of Trinidad. The indigenous population has been replaced by transplants, consisting of African slaves, indentured Indians, Chinese labourers and imported Europeans.

Amidst such heterogeneity therefore, a unitary and homogenous cultural identity is simply not possible in the case of Trinidadians. It is only natural that these displaced people, uprooted from their real homes, should find themselves out of place in an alien land. In Elbaki Hermassi's words:

> Displaced from their real homes and transported to distant lands, they experience a totally 'negative sense of place.' They are unable to possess in the spiritual sense the land they have in the physical sense.[4]

The degradation of their cultures together with the severe restrictions imposed on their life pattern in the colonies reduced them to virtual non-entities. It is against such a context that one must try to view the process of their coming into consciousness. In *Street* and *House*, Naipaul deals sensitively with the East Indians' struggle to find a foothold in the New World. Deeply involved in the colonized people's quest for order and identity, Naipaul makes these aspects central to his novels. He is particularly interested in the fate of the individuals in the colonial ethos, where the pressure exerted by the colonizing culture suppresses and distorts their identity. During the initial stages of cultural colonization, the colonized seem to react by showing a complete, surrender of the "self" to the "other," in a bid to win recognition. In this struggle, the colonized often felt that complete self-realization is not possible in a society that keeps pulling them back continuously. In *Passage*, Naipaul observes that individuals are forced to conform to the mediocrity of a society like Trinidad, which neither recognizes talent nor allows it to flourish. In such a society, people who possess unusual skills are often cut down to size or "made to boil down."[5] Placed in such a situation the talented and the gifted ones among the colonized were faced with the dilemma of either escaping from the society or fighting against the social order. Paradoxically, however, the quest for identity of the colonized was often expressed not through open assertion, but by a complete surrender of the "self" to the "other." In *Street*, Naipaul shows how limiting the environment in colonial societies can be while in *House*, he presents the individual's struggle against it.

Written in 1955, *Street* happens to be the first sustained work of Naipaul's. Yet, it was published much later, in 1959 and came third in the chronological order of publication, after *Masseur* and *Suffrage*. This study would consider Street in the order of its publication so as to maintain the overall sense of continuity in theme and setting that emerges from such a reading. For, while *Masseur* dealt with the rural world of Trinidad and *Suffrage* focused on its multiracial aspect, it is only logically correct that *Street* should be set in Port of Spain and add the third dimension to the picture of Trinidad. References within the text also support its placement as the third in the sequence. For instance, Ganesh from *Masseur* reappears in *Street* at the end. We are told that at the time Ganesh is still a minister, but "in the running for the M.B.E."[6] Again, Hat's lawyer, Chittaranjan is none other than the person mentioned in *Suffrage* as the Goldsmith's brother.

So far as the theme of cultural disintegration of the East Indian community is concerned, *Street* demonstrates the marginal position of the East Indians in the Creole dominated Port of Spain. The East Indians form a small minority in the *Street*. Bhaku's is the only other Indian family living in the *Street*, apart from the narrator and his mother. Then there is Bogart, who happens to be a real-life character as Naipaul has himself said. "By bringing the lonely, real-life character of Bogart into his fiction" writes Bibhu Padi of this character, "Naipaul was only restating the aimlessness, the rootless isolation of the Indians in the West Indies."[7] Bhaku, who belongs to an older generation of Indians, can sing verses from the Ramayana. Bhaku's wife proudly claims that her husband can read and write Hindi as well as English. When the narrator's mother tells her that Bhaku should get some work her reply is: "You could see *he* working with all the rude and crude people it have here in Port of Spain?"[8] It is clear that the Bhaku's maintain their distance from the Creole Negroes, who form the majority in the street. The tension that exists between the two races is made implicit. The narrator, however, being of a much younger generation and having grown up in the street feels no such inhibitions. However, when he falls into the typical vices of the street, and takes to drinking and visiting brothels, his mother rescues him from a life of total debauchery by sending him away to England to further his studies.

Street marks an important stage in Naipaul's development as a writer. Naipaul claims that it was through this book that he discovered "the trick of writing after a lot of fumbling..." (qtd. in Selwyn Cudjoe: 32). The episodic structure of the book is strongly reminiscent of his father's collection of short stories, *The Adventures of Gurudeva and other short stories*,[9] which Naipaul may have used as a model. The episodic structure perfectly fits Naipaul's purpose, which is to introduce us to the picaroon society of Port of Spain.

Street consists of seventeen loosely interlinked episodes, each of which focuses on one particular character inhabiting the street. *Street* is more a series of character sketches than a novel in the strict sense of having a single sustained plot. However, the episodes are held together by the common setting as well as the common first person narrator, through whose perspective we view the slum world of the street. In Francis Wyndham's words: "Unity of theme, mood, manners and background binds the stories ... so tightly that the collection is almost a novel."[10] The narrator, who has come to the street from Chaguanas, a year or two before the war, recounts things as they appeared to him as a boy living in the street. In the beginning, the narrator, merely a child, is awed and enchanted by the slum world. He even sees his role-model in Eddoes, the scavenging cart driver, who is also considered as one of the aristocrats of the street. However, at the end of the novel when as a boy of eighteen, the narrator begins to view things critically, the spell is broken and he sees the street for what it really is.

The major thematic concern of the novel is to convey the social realities of the urban world of colonial Trinidad. The episodes together complete the picture of a typical picaroon society, which has no set standards for anything. However, we find a natural sophistication and tolerance in the street life, which elicits a sympathetic response. Drawing attention to this aspect of the picaroon society of Trinidad in *Passage*, Naipaul observes:

> To condemn the picaroon society out of hand is to ignore its important quality. And this is not its ability to beguile and enchant. For if such a society breeds cynicism, it also breeds tolerance, not the tolerance between castes and creeds and so on—which does not exist in Trinidad anyway—but something more profound: tolerance for every human activity and affection for every demonstration of wit and style.[11]

We may disapprove of the unconventional behaviour of the residents of Miguel Street, at the same time however, we cannot remain untouched by their spirit of tolerance which accommodates everyone.

The residents of Miguel Street are natural eccentrics. In *Passage* Naipaul defines eccentricity as "the expression of one's own personality, unhampered by fear of ridicule or the discipline of a class."[12] It is through eccentric behaviour that the characters in *Street* seek to break the tedium of their lives and get noticed. The narrator sees the street as a world, where "everybody was quite different from everybody else."[13] Man-Man is mad; George, stupid; Big Foot, a bully; Hat, an adventurer; Popo, a philosopher and Morgan, a comedian. Yet in order to become an accepted member of the street gang it is necessary to have something in common. It is only when Popo, the carpenter, stops working, begins to get drunk and throw his temper around that he becomes acceptable. Though the variety of individual responses in the street seem to give the impression of individuality, however, the reality is far from this. The variety lies only in the masks of eccentricity that the residents of the street wear to get themselves noticed. This is not to say that the street is devoid of individuals with genuine yearnings. There are characters like Popo,

B. Wordsworth and Elias, who are not fakes, but their yearnings are sadly out of tune with their environment. Popo, the carpenter is a poetic man, who is "always busy hammering and sawing and planing."[14] His wish to be creative and original is evident in his untiring efforts to give shape to "the thing without a name," but when his wife elopes with another man, he is forced to become materialistic enough to steal and sell other's furniture after remodelling them. Elias wants to be a doctor, but ends up as a scavenging cart driver. B. Wordsworth, claims a spiritual kinship with the poet William Wordsworth and shares the latter's awe for nature. His secret ambition is to write the greatest poem in the world. His dream, however, remains unfulfilled because the only kind of poetry that finds appreciation in the street society is the kind contained in the Calypso, a purely Trinidadian song form which deals with local incidents and attitudes.[15]

Two characteristics about the social life of the Creole Negroes are especially noticeable in *Street*. First, their casual attitude to illegitimacy and second, the brutality towards women and children, both of which are the residual elements of their slave past. Though alongside legal marriage, the practice of having "keepers" was also prevalent among the Africans, it was due to slavery that the latter system became more common.[16] Denied of a family life during the days of slavery, the Negroes could only form casual relationships. On the other hand, physical brutality of the strong towards the weak being the basis of the slave system, it was also resorted to by the slaves as a means of psychological release and became a common feature of West Indian life.

Most of the man-woman relationships portrayed in *Street* are of a casual nature. In the first story entitled "Bogart," when Bogart suddenly disappears from the street, Hat and his friends begin to use Bogart's room as their club-house. They play cards, drink and even bring "the odd stray woman to the room."[17] Eddoes is caught off-guard when Bogart returns suddenly and discovers him with a woman. In "George and the Pink House," when George's wife dies, he simply brings another woman to stay with him and when she leaves him, he converts his house into a brothel and starts entertaining American soldiers. Hat voices the typical attitude to marriage in "until the soldiers came," when his brother, Edward says that he has to get married because his girlfriend is "making baby." Hat remarks scornfully:

> Is a damn funny thing to say. If everybody married because woman making baby for them it go be a hell of a thing. What happen that you want to be different now from everybody else in Trinidad? You come so American.[18]

Even among married couples, loyalty is a rare thing. In "The thing without a Name," Popo's wife elopes with the gardener of the big house where she works as a cook. She however, returns to Popo after he has painted and furnished his house. Hat's comment draws attention to the materialistic tendencies of the society: "I bet you if the man in Arima had a new house and new furnitures, she wouldnta come back with Popo."[19] The case of Mrs. Hereira in "Love, Love, Love, Alone" is somewhat different. She also leaves her husband for a man called Toni. However, it is not for money, but for love. When it is discovered that Mrs. Hereira is actually the wife of Mr. Christiani, a wealthy doctor, Hat wonders why she ever left her husband for a man like Toni, who only abuses her. It is probably because her wealthy husband neglects her that she looks elsewhere for love and attention. When Toni begins to drink and abuse her and even threatens to kill her, she is forced to return to her husband and settle for the comforts without love.

In *Street*, child-beating and woman-battering is a common everyday affair. For George, it is a recreational activity, entertaining enough to keep him from joining the street gang:

> George never became one of the gang in Miguel Street. He didn't seem to mind. He had his wife and his daughter and his son. He beat them all. And when the boy Elias grew too big, George beat his daughter and his wife more than ever.[20]

For Bhaku, beating his wife is a ritual. He uses a cricket bat for the purpose and Mrs. Bhaku herself keeps the bat well-oiled and ready for use. In the Indian context also wife-beating is accepted as the husband's prerogative. The general attitude is summed up in the Calypso:

> Every now and then just knock them down,
> Every now and then just throw them down,
> Black up their eye and bruise up their knee,
> And then they love you eternally.[21]

Children are treated no better. When the narrator and Hat's nephews, Boyee and Errol, are together they compare notes about beatings and Boyee says: "The blows we get is nothing to what Big Foot used to get from his father."[22] Hat supplements the information:

> Every day Big Foot father, the policeman, giving Big Foot blows. Like medicine. Three times a day after meals. And hear Big Foot talk afterwards. He used to say, when I get big and have children, I go beat them, beat them.[23]

The narrator's comment provides a psychological insight as to how brutality becomes self perpetuating: "I didn't say it then, because I was ashamed; but I had often felt the same way when my mother beat me."[24]

Though there is much laughter in *Street*, the stories demonstrate that the world is a "stupid, sad place," and the narrator realises this through Laura, the prostitute. She is the most vivacious and gay person in the street, but when Laura's eldest daughter comes home one night and tells her—"Ma, I going to make baby,"[25] Laura's defences crumble and she begins to cry. The narrator's comment shows that laughter is one of the masks of bravado that each character wears to hide the bitter reality of their lives:

> And for the first time I heard Laura crying. It wasn't ordinary crying. She seemed to be crying all the cry she had saved up since she was born; all the cry she had tried to cover up with her laughter.[26]

Naipaul, in an interview with Frank Winstone, observed "If through the comedy you can't see the central tragedy, then the comedy isn't very good" (qtd. in Landeg White: 33). Even amidst the boisterous laughter, Naipaul never allows us to loose sight of the central tragedy in the lives of the residents of Miguel Street. It is exemplified in the case of Dolly, George's daughter. In spite of being beaten up by her father, Dolly is always giggling. Even the day she gets married, George tells her jocularly: "Dolly, you married, it true. But don't think you too big for me to put you across my lap and cut your tail."[27] There is a great deal of laughter among the guests. An American soldier, who is drunk tells George: "You could put this girl to better work, George."[28] Though every body laughs, Dolly bursts into tears, deeply insulted by the innuendo.

An idea that is frequently expressed in *Street* is the inadequacy of the colonial society that requires no efficiency. Popo, the carpenter is never idle but when the narrator asks him what he is making, his reply is: "Ha, boy! that's the question, I making the thing without a name."[29] When his signboard attracts customers, he panics and misdirects them: "The carpenter fellow?" "He don't live here again."[30] This aspect is highlighted in the narrator's comment regarding Big Foot's casual change in profession from a carpenter to a mason: "There is no stupid pride among Trinidad craftsmen. No one is a specialist."[31]

To the residents of Miguel Street, England and America are the only places where any thing of worth is possible. When somebody has the idea of organising a "Local Talent on Parade Show," Edward comments sarcastically: "Don't make me laugh. What sort of talent they think Trinidad have."[32] Admiration for America is the latest craze and everyone tries to emulate American mannerisms. When Bogart returns, after disappearing for the second time, the narrator notices Bogart's deliberate imitation of American behaviour patterns:

> His accent was now pure American. To complete the imitation, he began being expansive towards children. He called out to them in the streets, and gave them money to buy gum and chocolate. He loved stroking their heads, and giving them good advice.[33]

During the Second World War when the American soldiers flood Trinidad, Edward stops working in the cow-pen and gets a job with the Americans in chaguanas. He is full of praise for the Americans: "And the Americans not like the British, you know. They does make you work hard, but they does pay for it."[34] His complete surrender to the Americans makes him drift away from the street gang, which saddens the narrator. A complete change comes over Edward's dress habits and attitude:

> He began wearing clothes in the American style, he began chewing gum, and tried to talk with an American accent. We didn't see much of him except on Sundays, and then he made us feel small and inferior.[35]

By the end of the novel, there is a complete change even in the narrator's attitude to Trinidad. When his mother rebukes him for his wild dissolute ways, he blames Trinidad for it: "Is not my fault really. Is just Trinidad. What else anybody can do here except drink?"[36] It seems that the only hope lies in escape from Trinidad. *Streets* also ends on the note of rejection with the narrator's departure to London.

Naipaul's creative genius is evident even in his first book, in the expert handling of the narrative technique. By exploiting the single first person narrator's dual perspectives, as a child and as a grown-up recalling his childhood, Naipual is able to re-create his childhood experience and at the same time avoid making judgements. The ironic gap between the child's innocent view of things and the critical but detached account of the grown-up narrator recalling his boyhood experiences is enough to convey the true picture. As Madhusudana Rao observes "Miguel Street...emerges as a symbol of the tragic-comic situation of man in the new world environment."[37] As opportunity does not lend itself to ambition, the residents of Miguel Street can do little more than take refuge in fantasy. In an amoral and tolerant society that lays no standards, personality cannot crystallize into a meaningful entity but remains fluid and shapeless. Consequently, the quests for meaning carried out within the society end in failure. The only success story of Miguel Street is the narrator's, which also is a story of escape. For a success story within the limiting environment of Trinidad we must turn to Naipaul's next novel, *House*. While the preceding novels examined the social and political aspects of colonial Trinidad, *House* delves deeper into the psyche of an individual to reveal the major problematic of the dispossessed individual—the carving of an authentic selfhood.

There is an essential difference in approach between the other novels and *House*. The first three novels end on a negative note with the protagonists' rejection of their societies whereas *House* endorses a positive approach to the problem of displacement. Mr. Biswas, in *House* tries to overcome the limitations imposed on him by putting up a relentless struggle against the forces that try to suppress his individuality. His struggle is a long and traumatic one but he is successful in his negotiation for space and finally fulfils his dream of having a house of his own, which is a stupendous achievement for a man of his limited and mediocre circumstances. As against the heroes and antiheroes of the earlier novels, who finally rejected their society, Mr. Biswas represents the multitudes who endured and made it home. It is in a truer sense the social history of the East Indians in Trinidad. *House* is epic in scope and tells the story of Mohan Biswas from birth to death. Divided into manageable sections, the story moves forward progressively and each section deals with a different phase of Biswas's life. While cultural clash and the gradual disintegration of the East Indian community still forms the major preoccupation in the novel, Naipaul, at the same time focuses on the related problem of the East Indians' finding a foothold in the New World.

The first section of the novel called "Pastorals" describes the birth and childhood years of Biswas. In this section the Hindu way of life finds its fullest expression in the customs, traditions, rituals and the social philosophy of the people. This section of the novel represents Indians like Bipti's father, who came to Trinidad as indentured labourers and reproduces the India that they had created for themselves. There is a vivid representation of the complete communal life, which is made evident through their superstitious beliefs, their faith in the pundit, the customs and rituals they still follow and above all in their belief in preordination.

When Bissoondaye, Biswas's grandmother, learns that Biswas is born the wrong way and is six-fingered it is past midnight. Even then, superstitious as she is, she walks to the next village to get leaves of cactus, which she cuts into strips and hangs on every door, window and aperture she can find in order to ward-off evil spirits. A pundit is immediately called in to see Biswas's horoscope. The Pundit consults his astrological almanac, predicts that Biswas will have the "unlucky sneeze" and prescribes: "much of the evil this boy will undoubtedly bring will be mitigated if his father is forbidden to see him for twenty-one days."[38] The pundit even gives a detailed instruction as to how Biswas's father must take his first look at his son:

> You must fill this brass plate with coconut oil—which by the way, you must make yourself from coconuts you have collected with your own hands and in the reflection on this oil the father must see his son's face.[39]

Bissoondaye follows the Pundit's instructions diligently and on the twenty-first day Raghu has his first view of his son. Nevertheless, Biswas proves unlucky for his father and becomes the cause of his death. Bipti undergoes her initiation into widowhood in the traditional manner. The ritual is described in detail:

> Bipti was bathed. Her hair, still wet, was neatly parted and then filled with red henna. Then the henna was scooped out and the parting filled with charcoal dust. She was now a widow forever.[40]

In addition to the observance of traditional customs and rituals, the East Indians have also retained their belief in preordination. This is first expressed by Bipti's father when she tells him about her unhappy marriage with Raghu and he tries to console her by saying: "Fate, there is nothing we can do about it."[41] It is also evident in the narrator himself, who makes the following observation about Bipti's father: "Fate had brought him from India to the sugar-estate, aged him quickly and left him to die in a crumbling mud hut in the swamp lands."[42] Bipti too, shows a passive resignation to fate till the end. The insularity of the East Indians is evidenced even in the fact that they have retained the use of Hindi. This becomes apparent during Raghu's funeral when Tara, Bipti's sister, has to translate into Hindi what the photographer says in English. In spite of the insularity of the East Indians, however, the intrusion of the alien environment is already making itself felt. These Trinidad Hindus are forced to change their traditional custom and bury instead of cremating their dead. Raghu has to be buried, and later Biswas's own cremation "one of the few permitted by the Health Department,"[43] is conducted on the banks of a muddy stream.

After Raghu's death, Biswas and Bipti have to move to Pagotes and live as dependents on Tara, Bipti's well-to-do sister. The move to Pagotes is significant because it is at this point that the fragmentation of Biswas's life begins as the following passage reveals:

> And so Mr. Biswas came to leave the only house to which he had some right. For the next thirty-five years he was to be a wanderer with no place he could call his own, with no family except that which he was to attempt to create out of the engulfing world of the Tulsis. For with his mother's parents dead, his brother on the estate at Felicity, Dehuti as a servant in Tara's house, and himself rapidly growing away from Bipti who, broken, became increasingly useless and impenetrable, it seemed to him that he was really quite alone.[44]

In Pagotes, Biswas and his mother live in a back trace sharing a mud hut with some of Tara's husband's dependent relations, who remain strangers to them. After coming to Pagotes they live completely on Tara's charity. Bipti loses her hold over Biswas as now it is Tara who decides everything for them. It is Tara, who sends Biswas to the Canadian Mission school, and then suddenly decides that he should be made a pundit. So, he is sent to Pundit Jairam to receive his training. Pundit Jairam is a strange man who holds scandalous views and is full of contradictions:

> He believed in God, fervently, but claimed it was not necessary for a Hindu to do so. He attacked the custom some families had of putting up a flag after a religious ceremony; but his own front garden was a veritable grove of bamboo poles with red and white pennants in varying stages of decay. He ate no meat but spoke against vegetarianism: when Lord Rama went hunting, did they think it was just for sport?[45]

Biswas spends eight months with this eccentric man, doing "the mechanical side of Jairam's offices"[46] and copying out "Sanskrit verses, which he couldn't understand."[47] After some time, Biswas is thrown out by Jairam because of a disgraceful act on his part. He returns to Pagotes expecting his mother to welcome and console him, but Bipti, who depends on Tara's bounty can only express her own apprehensions: "And it was Tara who wanted you to be a pundit." She tells Biswas: "I don't know what we are going to tell her."[48] When Tara is told, she again sends Biswas away to help at her husband's rum shop, which is being looked after by Bhandat, her brother-in-law. Bipti, who is never consulted, is grateful and even Biswas is happy at the prospect of earning two dollars a month. However, Bhandat considers Biswas as Tara's spy and takes a dislike for him. He accuses Biswas of stealing a dollar, beats him up and turns him out. Biswas returns once again and in his humiliation cries out pathetically, to his mother: "why do you keep on sending me to stay with other people."[49] It is then that Biswas, for the first time, declares his resolution to have his own house, which for him has become a symbol of liberation: I am going to get a job of my own. And am going to get my own house too. I am finished with this.[50]

After making the declaration of independence Biswas takes up sign painting and also develops the hobby of reading. He becomes addicted to Samuel smiles and tries to identify with the heroes who, like himself, are young, poor and struggling. Yet, he realizes the vast difference between his condition and their's. While he lived in a place where there could be no place for ambition, they inhabited a land of possibilities where "ambitions could be pursued and had a meaning."[51] Biswas realizes that there is little he can do besides "opening a shop or buying a motorbus."[52] The idea that colonial people are condemned to mediocrity underlies most of Naipauls writings. Biswas, nevertheless tries to rise above this mediocrity by trying to invent things. He buys seven expensive volumes of *Hawkins' Electrical Guide*, but cannot go beyond making rudimentary items like doorbells and buzzers, not because he is incapable but simply because Trinidad cannot furnish him with the equipment necessary to carry out more complex experiments as the narrator points out:

> He bought the seven expensive volumes of Hawkins' Electrical Guide, made rudimentary compasses, buzzers and doorbells, and learned to wind an armature. Beyond that he could not go. Experiments became more complex, and he didn't know where in Trinidad he could find the equipment mentioned so casually by Hawkins. His interest

> in electrical matters died, and he contented himself with reading about the Samuel Smiles heroes in their magic land.[53]

Yet, Biswas does not lose heart. He remains firm on his belief that "he lived in a land where romance was possible."[54] In no other character of Naipaul's do we find such a profound optimism and faith in life. Referring to Biswas's unquenchable hope, Kenneth Ramchand observes:

> But if Mr. Biswas finds his world a deterrent to ambition, as well as engulfing and repulsive, the faith in life with which his author endows him...is greater than the fictional character's impulse to escape.[55]

In the early section of the novel, the Hindu social order predominates. Yet, a close reading reveals that the process of disintegration has already begun to set in due to forces operating both within as well as outside it. In the character of Lal, a low caste Hindu converted to Presbyterianism, there is an oblique reference to the threat posed by such conversions to other religions. The rigidity of the Hindu social order is threatened from within by intercaste marriages like the one between Biswas's sister Dehuti and Ramchand, a low caste Hindu. At this stage, such marriages are strongly disapproved and the couple, being ostracized by the society, have to shift to Port of Spain. Later, however, such marriages become socially sanctioned as is evident in the arranged marriage between Shekar, Mrs. Tulsi's elder son and Dorothy, who belongs to a Presbyterian family. The disintegration is also visible in casual inter-racial liaisons like the one between Bhandat and a Chinese woman. Though these are peripheral cases, yet, they signify the beginning of the process of disintegration of the rigid norms which governed the East Indian society.

Naipaul never loses sight of the catalytic role played by education in bringing about the disintegration of the East Indian community. Maureen Warner-Lewis, a critic commenting on the effects of formal education on traditional culture, observes: "One of the main reasons for the disintegrating influence of formal education on tradition is that the topics treated in the system are European."[56] She also points out that there is a divorce between "the school inspired formal ideal on the one hand and the real and local on the other."[57] It is the description of foreign landscapes he has read about in his school books that makes Biswas imagine his dream house with a bower, which is incompatible with the arid tropical island he actually lives in. This reflects the subtle way in which education moulds the tastes of the colonized people. In *Passage* drawing attention to this aspect of Trinidad, Naipaul observes:

> This was the taste of the old Trinidad: individual, anarchic, not arising out, of the place—in spite of the fireplaces every office in white hall needs two or three fans—but created out of memories.[58]

In the Canadian Mission school, Biswas learns about things as irrelevant to him as "geysers, rift valley, watersheds, currents, the Gulf Stream and a number of deserts."[59] The history taught in the school is "a discipline as unreal as the geography."[60] History that is immediately and directly relevant to the Trinidadians is deliberately neglected and it is only from his friend Alec, that Biswas first hears about the Great War.

The next section of the novel marks a yet another important phase of Biswas's life in which his epic struggle with the Tulsi clan begins. It is his sign-painting that brings Biswas into contact with Hanuman House, where he is trapped into a modern marriage without any dowry and is expected to become a tulsi because he has "no money or position."[61] Biswas is expected to merge into insignificance like the other sons-in-law, some of whose names even have been forgotten. When Govind, one of the sons-in-law, suggests that Biswas should give up sign-painting and become a driver in the Tulsi estate, Biswas immediately voices his dissent: "Give up sign-painting? And my independence? No, boy. My motto is: paddle your own canoe."[62] Biswas thus comes to be regarded with hostility and ridiculed as "Biswas the paddler." As Gordon Rohlehr points out "Tulsidom depends for its existence on the psychic emasculation of the men and on the maintenance of their sense of inferiority."[63] Biswas, however refuses to join the herd and adopts a combative stance from the very beginning. To spite the Tulsis, he joins the Aryans, a group of revisionist Hindu Missionaries from India, and proselytises for them by advocating girls' education, abolition of child marriage, caste system and idol worship. He preaches against all the doctrines the Tulsis hold dear. Mrs. Tulsi is particularly displeased because Owad, her younger son is trying to get into the Catholic College and she fears that Biswas's involvement with the Aryans may create problems for Owad.

About this time, the uncertainty and inconsequentiality of his life begins to dawn upon Biswas. He realizes that he has achieved nothing in life. He reflects:

> Suppose that at one word I could just disappear from this room, what would remain to speak of me? A few clothes, a few books. The shouts and thumps in the hall would continue; the puja would be done; in the morning the Tulsi store would open its doors.[64]

The insight makes him even more quarrelsome. On one occasion he goes to the extent of spitting on Owad, for which he is beaten up by Govind and sent away to The Chaze. Moving away from Hanuman House with a pregnant Shama is a personal triumph for Biswas. It is also significant because; it demonstrates the fact that the conformity which an extended family system demands is no longer possible in the changing environment, where people have begun to assert their individuality. By breaking away from the Tulsi household, Biswas has introduced into the feudal world of the Tulsis the capitalistic concept of "the freedom of choice." In the Tulsi household itself, which is made out to be conservative, there are clear signs of cultural confusion. This is at once evident in the Crucifix that Shekhar wears, which undoubtedly is the influence of the Roman Catholic College he attends. However, the rest of the Tulsis also regard the Crucifix as "an exotic and desirable charm."[65]

In the section entitled "The chaze" Biswas begins an independent life with Shama. From the beginning, however, Biswas has the feeling that The chaze is just a temporary arrangement and "real life was to begin for them soon and elsewhere. The chaze was a pause a preparation."[66] Naipaul diagnoses the feeling of temporariness to be a typical condition among the displaced people. Even Hanuman House, for all its apparent solidity is actually built of clay bricks, the reason being that "the Tulsis had never considered themselves settled in Arwacas or even Trinidad. It was no more than a stage in the journey that had begun when Pundit Tulsi left India."[67] The old men who assemble in the arcade of Hanuman House continually talk of returning to India. However, when the opportunity to go back to India does come, they are afraid to leave the "familiar temporariness" of Trinidad. What has happened in the meanwhile is that without realizing it these East Indians have developed ties with Trinidad. Biswas never gets over the feeling of temporariness throughout the period he spends at The Chaze.

Importantly, after coming to The Chaze, Biswas's attitude to Hanuman House changes. He realizes that though Hanuman House had seemed chaotic to him, it was in reality ordered. He discovers that "the House was a world, more real than The Chaze, and less exposed; everything beyond its gates were foreign and unimportant."[68] His loneliness at The Chaze makes him recall the warmth and noisy activity of Hanuman House, where in spite of all the hostility he had been acknowledged at least as a clown. At The Chaze he feels reduced to a non-entity. What Naipaul seeks to convey is that one's sense of identity is rooted in relationships, the denial of which can only lead to alienation. When Biswas realizes that Hanuman House is a sanctuary he needs, his relationship with the Tulsis undergoes a change. He visits Hanuman House more often and even tries to win their favour. Nevertheless, a vague sense of desolation and uncertainty still haunts him and heightens the tensions between him and Shama. Biswas's fear and uncertainty have to be understood in psychic terms. His fears are the fears of a man who has yet to find his place in an environment that disowns him. The crisis within Biswas finds an apt expression in his vision of the boy he had chanced to see while conducting one of Ajodha's buses:

> It was late afternoon and they were racing back along the ill-made country road. Their lights were weak and they were racing the sun. The sun fell; and in the short dusk they passed a lonely hut set in a clearing far back from the road. Smoke came from under the ragged thatched eaves: the evening meal was being prepared. And, in the gloom, a boy was leaning against the hut,

> his hands behind him, staring at the road. He wore a vest and nothing more. The vest glowed white. In an instant the bus went by, noisy in the dark, through bush and level sugar-cane fields. Mr. Biswas could not remember where the hut stood, but the picture remained: a boy leaning against an earth house that had no reason for being there, under the dark, falling sky, a boy who didn't know where the road and that bus went.[69]

The picture keeps recurring to Biswas at crucial moments and counters the house metaphor, which signifies light, order and security. Shama, ensconced as she has been in Hanuman House experiences no such crisis. Biswas's first attempt to Paddle his own canoe meets with failure when his shop incurs heavy losses and he is forced to accept the job of a sub-overseer at a salary of twenty-five dollars, in one of the Tulsi estates.

Life at the barracks in Green vale is a harrowing experience for Biswas. After the spacious accommodation at The Chaze, the single room into which he moves in with family and furniture leaves him feeling suffocated. His claustrophobia develops into a general phobia for people. Though Biswas had resolved to start building his house immediately after coming to Green Vale he once again lapses into inaction. On one of his visits to Hanuman House he sees Anand standing against the pillars and is reminded of the other boy he had seen outside the hut at dusk. The vision sets Biswas into action and his house begins to take shape in reality. Biswas's first attempt to claim a portion of the earth fails to bear fruit. The house meets the same end as the doll's house he had gifted his daughter Savi on her birthday and outraged Mrs. Tulsi by the reiteration of his independence. Shama had had to break the house in order to pacify her people. The house Biswas starts building at Green Vale can in no way be an embodiment of his aspirations, for Biswas is still dependent on the Tulsis. Besides, financial constraints compel him to make compromises, so that the house he manages to get constructed bears no resemblance to his dream house. This explains the apathy that settles upon him soon after the construction begins. The intensity of the alienation he experiences is reflected in his conversation with his son:

> 'Who is your father?'
>
> 'You,'
>
> 'Wrong. I am not your father. God is your father.'
>
> 'Oh, And what about you?'
>
> 'I am just somebody. Nobody at all. I am just a man you know.'[70]

Biswas moves into the finished room of his house in a defiant gesture with the hope that living in his own house would bring about a change in the state of his mind. However, When Tarzan, his dog, is brutally killed presumably by the dispossessed labourers, Biswas is badly shaken and feels more threatened than ever. The same day he has a nervous breakdown. Biswas finds himself once again in Hanuman House, where he is nursed back to health. When he recovers, Seth breaks the news to Biswas that his house has been burnt down by the labourers. Biswas is immensely relieved by the news, for he can never think of going back to the house after the horrifying experience he has had. The one positive outcome of the time spent at Green Vale is that Biswas is able to claim his children, Savi and Anand, who had here-to-fore been the assets only of Hanuman House.

On recovering, Biswas reviews his situation once again and finds that "his position was as it had been when he was seventeen, unmarried and ignorant of the Tulsis,"[71] but when he measures this unhappiness against the agony and despair experienced in Green Vale, he feels greatly relieved. An inertia settles upon him once again. He is goaded into action when Seth tells him that Mrs. Tulsi and Owad are expected back from Port of Spain, which means that he must vacate Owad's room. Biswas leaves quietly without seeing Shama and his fourth child. When Biswas sets out he has no idea where he is to go or what he is to do. It is quite by chance that he gets into a bus going to Port of Spain and ends up as a journalist.

We get further evidence of the disintegration of Hanuman House in the final section of the first part of the novel. It is to be seen in their celebration of Christmas, but more definitely in the arranged marriage between Shekar and Dorothy. When a beautiful, educated and rich girl cannot be found in the same caste Mrs. Tulsi is ready to settle for any Hindu girl who satisfies the required qualifications. However, when no Hindu girl fitting the description can be found, they ultimately settle for a girl, who belongs to "a laxly presbyterian family, with one filling station, two lorries, a cinema and some land."[72] We cannot miss the change in the priorities. Caste, till then the prime consideration, has now been replaced by pecuniary factors. Shekar's marriage takes place in a registry office after which instead of bringing the bride home, it is Shekhar who leaves Hanuman House to "look after the lorries, Cinema, land and the filling station of his wife's family."[73] Even within Hanuman House, the crack-up begins to show in the quarrels that ensue after Mrs. Tulsi and Owad leave for Port of Spain where Owad is to continue his studies:

> During her absences the accepted degrees of precedence at Hanuman House lost some of their meaning. Sushila, the widow, was reduced to nonentity. Many sisters attempted to seize power and a number of squabbles ensued. Offended sisters ostentatiously looked after their own families, sometimes even cooking separately for a day or two. Padma, Seth's wife, alone continued to be respected, but she showed no inclination to assert authority. Seth exacted the obedience of everyone; he could not impose harmony. That was re-established every week-end when Mrs. Tulsi and the younger god returned.[74]

It is apparent that beneath the community life of Hanuman House, there are individualistic tendencies, which are only held in check by Mrs. Tulsi. These instances foretell its complete collapse that would eventually occur at Shorthills.

The second part of the novel mainly focuses on Port of Spain where Mrs. Tulsi and Owad have shifted and where Biswas also arrives after leaving Hanuman House. Port of Spain provides Biswas the foothold he has long been in search of. His sign painting opens the way for a job at the "Trinidad Sentinel," where he is taken in as a reporter at a salary of fifteen dollars a month. Apart from establishing his identity as a person in his own right, the job also changes the attitude of the Tulsis towards him, so that when their reconciliation takes place it is "on terms that made Biswas feel he had won a victory."[75] Mrs. Tulsi offers Biswas two rooms in her house in Port of Spain, which he accepts considering it the climax of his good fortune. His relations with Mrs. Tulsi becomes less formal while a sweet companionship grows between him and Owad. At the home front, Biswas sets about "establishing his tyrannies"[76] as the head of the family and even Shama on her rare visits to Hanuman House can proudly boast that "the children are afraid of him."[77] Biswas himself begins to feel that his household has at last been established. At times, he even forgets that the house belongs to the Tulsi's as the rose bush he plants in the garden testifies. However Biswas's idyllic life is cut short by a number of events. The sudden takeover of the "Trinidad sentinel" by new authorities after the equally abrupt dismissal of Mr. Burnett, the editor, poses a new threat to Biswas. Seth's break-up with the Tulsis and Mrs. Tulsi's subsequent decision to shift to Shorthills also comes as a blow to Biswas upsetting his routine once again.

At shorthills, with no Seth to supervise over the Tulsis, the split-up is complete. They are no longer united or organised as they had been at Hanuman House. Here, in Shorthills, it is each man to himself and everyone tries to exploit the resources to his own advantage. The new order that has emerged at Shorthills is based not on co-operation but on competition. Govind and Tuttle are foremost in the plundering:

> Then the news of the ravages of W.C. Tuttle and Govind was whispered through the house. W.C. Tuttle had been selling whole Cedar trees. Govind had been selling lorry loads, of oranges and papaws and avocado pears and limes and grapefruit and cocoa and tonka beans.[78]

Biswas too takes advantage of his stay at Shorthills which for him is "an insurance against the sack" and "an opportunity to save, an opportunity to plunder."[79] Disunity sets in among the children as well and this is reflected in their "bitter fights of pure hate."[80] It is clear to the Tulsis that "there was no longer a Hanuman House to protect them; everyone had to fight for himself in a new world, the world Owad and Shekhar had entered, where education was the only protection."[81] So, there is a frantic scramble for education among the Tulsis. About this time, Hari, the family Pundit passes away. This is a great blow to the Tulsis, for there is no one to take his place and though Mrs. Tulsi continues to hold pujas, it is without the feasting and gaiety which characterised such ceremonies at Hanuman House and as no other pundit can please Mrs. Tulsi after Hari's death, her faith too yields. The assimilation into the Creole culture is complete when Mrs. Tulsi starts sending Sushila to burn candles in the Roman Catholic Church, puts a crucifix in her room and has pundit Tulsi's grave cleaned for All Saint's Day.

At Shorthills, Biswas's ambition of having his own house finally finds fulfilment. Having saved a considerable amount of money while at Shorthills, he is able to complete the house within a short period and even shift into it. Yet, even this house has to be abandoned because of its inconvenient location. Though Biswas's ambition had remained steady, his circumstances had changed and the house had some practical problems:

> He had built his own house, in a place as wild and out-of-the-way as he could have wished. But Shama had to walk a mile to the village to do her shopping, water had to be brought up the hill from a spring in the cocoa woods. And there was the problem of transport. He had to cycle long distances every day, and though he had cut himself off from the family, his children had to go to school in the family car.[82]

Built in the wilderness, the new house imprisoned them in silence and bush. Even inside the house the children felt threatened by the smell of snakes and 'the nights seemed longer and blacker.'[83]

Biswas waits to be released from the house which cannot be a home to them and when Mrs. Tulsi once again offers him two rooms in the Port of Spain house, he readily accepts. In spite of all the negative aspects, however, it is in this house that for the first time the Biswases live together as a family. The experience of living together all by themselves adds a new dimension to Biswas's ambition. The house at Shorthills was the result of Biswas's personal ambition and fulfilled only his individual aspirations. Biswas now realizes that he has the responsibilities of a father and husband as well and that his ambition can become truly meaningful only if the aspirations of the other members of the family are also accommodated.

After the Shorthills interlude, Biswas once again returns to the Port of Spain house which he now has to share with some of the other Tulsis, like Govind, Tuttle and their families. In this section of the novel the sudden economic boom created by the American presence is evidenced in the way people like Govind and Tuttle become suddenly rich. As the narrator points out:

> There was money in the island. It showed in the suits of Govind, who drove the Americans in his taxi; in the possession of W.C. Tuttle who hired out his lorry to them; in the new cars; the new buildings.'[84]

We learn in the epilogue that even the Welfare Department is finally abolished because the "awareness of America had given everyone the urge and many the means to self-improvement. The encouragement and guidance of the department were no longer needed."[85]

However, despite the economic boom, Biswas's economic position remains unchanged because he does not have access to the kind of money people like Govind and Tuttle have come by. Biswas continues to live in the Port of Spain house even after Owad returns from England. Owad's return revives the community life of the Tulsis when even communal cooking is resumed, but there is still a competition among the sisters, with each sister trying to establish her intimacy with Owad. For a while things go well, then one day, Owad slaps Anand for answering back and in his humiliation Anand appeals to Biswas: "We must move. I can't bear to live here another day."[86] Biswas, who has himself faced such insults innumerable times since his childhood, is deeply moved by his son's appeal; and in his own helplessness creates a scene. On the same night Biswas insults Mrs. Tulsi and even tells her that he would be vacating her house. Having committed himself Biswas sets about looking for a rentable accommodation but fails to find a suitable one. With a saving that hardly amounts to eight hundred dollars it is impossible for him to even think of buying a house, but when he gets four hundred dollars for his Shorthills house, he is in a position to give it a serious thought. He manages a loan of four thousand dollars from Ajodha and finally decides to purchase the solicitor's clerk's house in Port of Spain.

Biswas's decision to move away from the Tulsis is met with opposition by Shama. Though she too is pained by Anand's humiliation, she is reluctant to leave the security of her family. Even when she is taken to view the house, she remains in a sullen mood, but surprisingly enough when the move is finally effected, she settles down in no time. After moving into the house, the Biswases discover its many flaws and realize that they have been cheated. Nevertheless, the fact that it is their own house makes them accommodate themselves "to every peculiarity and awkwardness of the house."[87] Shama's new-found loyalties become evident in the way she prepares the house to receive the Tuttles, she even tells them "I don't want anything bigger. This is just right for me. Something small and nice."[88] Biswas too learns to reciprocate the feeling of love. In Madhusudana Rao's words:

> In his own house, which is incomplete like his own syncopated individuality, he has come to respect the feeling of love,—that state of consciousness which recognizes the value of gifting one's self away to meet another's human need. In a sense, Mr. Biswas has at last arrived.[89]

Naipaul makes it clear that for displaced people like the Biswases, owning a house does not just mean having a shelter. It means the imposition of an order into their chaotic and patternless existence. It signifies stability and coherence, which are the pre-requisites for the carving of an authentic selfhood.

After the Biswases shift to their own house, there is a further change of scene in the Tulsi household. Following the unpleasantness with Biswas, Owad becomes reticent and isolates himself from the rest of the family and no amount of coaxing on Mrs. Tulsi's part can win him back. He starts spending most of his time away from home, with his medical colleagues, who form "a new caste separate from the society from which it had been released."[90] His assimilation into the wider society of Trinidad is complete when he gives up his job at the colonial hospital, and starts private practice in San Fernando. Though Mrs. Tulsi's death is not directly mentioned, it can be gathered in the epilogue from what the narrator says about Shama's sisters, who attend Biswas's funeral: "They all came. For them it was an occasion of reunion, no longer so frequent, for they had all moved to their own houses, some in town, some in the country."[91] The move must have taken place after Mrs. Tulsis demise. Biswas's own death is given the least importance. The emphasis lies elsewhere. What is more important is that Biswas has died an accommodated man, who has been successful in claiming a portion of the earth as his own and in leaving behind a proof of his existence. It is in the dignity of his death, that Biswas's triumph lies.

House marks the culmination of the early phase of Naipaul's development as a novelist. Landeg White notes the masterly handling of the comprehensive material: "Biswas is only forty-six when he dies, but by the end of the novel a whole history has passed before our eyes."[92] Compared to the preceding three novels, *House* demonstrates a fullness of character development. Naipaul's handling of Biswas's character is such that the readers are drawn into an intimacy with him. This becomes possible because every little incident in Biswas's life, his every thought and every single possession is known to the reader. With no other character is the identification as complete as it is with Biswas. While Ganesh in *Masseur* evokes sympathy initially, his characterization precludes intimacy. Naipaul's triumph lies in the fact that he has been able to present a hero "in all his littleness, and still preserve a sense of the man's inner dignity."[93] Viewed against the background of the society, as explored in the three preceding novels, Biswas's achievement appears heroic. In the final analysis we may make common cause with Francis Wyndham and say that "A House for Mr. Biswas is as subtle and comprehensive an analysis of the colonial situation as anything in imaginative literature."[94]

There is a general agreement among critics that Hanuman House is a miniature version of the plantation system introduced by the colonizers. The description of the organization of Hanuman House, in the novel, justifies the analogy:

> The organization of the Tulsi House was simple. The daughters and their children swept and washed and cooked and served in the store. The husbands, under Seth's supervision, worked on the Tulsi land, looked after the Tulsi animals, and served in the store. In return they were given food, shelter and a little money; their children were looked after....[95]

Naipaul also describes the joint family in which he grew up as "a microcosm of the authoritarian state, where power is all important."[96] However, we cannot forget that the principles on which Hanuman House functions are also the principles, of the traditional extended family system. Naipaul seems to suggest that traditional institutions like the extended family are equally responsible for perpetuating dependence and passivity by suppressing individuality and are major deterrents to the development of personality. It is significant that the process of Biswas's development into an individual in his own right is directly proportional to the process of disintegration of the Hindu social order. As the inherited order passes away, the self evolves into a new entity which is more viable to the new environment. Biswas must be shorn of his cultural identity and completely depersonalized before he can evolve into a new entity. Biswas reaches the "zero state of his cultural identity,"[97] when in spite of being a Brahmin by caste he is sent to the Sudra world of The Chaze to work as a labourer. The cultural void that he experiences leads to his nervous breakdown. However, this shearing of the cultural identity has been necessary to prepare Biswas to face the changing environment, where it is no longer possible to remain tethered to traditional caste roles.

Biswas's struggle for individuality raises questions about the basis and meaning of personality, out of which an interesting ambivalence emerges. The individual remains dependent on the society for his sense of being. Paradoxically however, it is necessary to rebel against the society in order to forge an authentic personality. As Gordon Rohlehr points out: "It is out of this confrontation that the new personality grows."[98]

It has been said about Naipaul's early novels, that in writing them he was writing-off his debts to his origins, before severing his "umbilical cord" with India. Rather than a writing-off, Naipaul's early novels were the outcome of his attempts to discover his identity and understand his own place in the world. It is Naipaul's "complex fate," that despite his multiple heritage, he is yet to find his spiritual home, and his writing emanates from his desire to come to terms with his own displacement and homelessness. For Naipaul, at every stage of his literary career, writing is an activity that leads to self discovery. He has himself said: "Most imaginative writers discover themselves, and their world, through their work."[99] Naipaul's quest for his identity has been brilliantly summed up in his words: "I didn't know who I was." It was writing which imposed an order on his experience and lent it coherence. Through an imaginative recreation of the past, he was able to reconcile himself to his present. Just as the house imposed a sense of order on the lives of the Biswases, the process of recording his ancestry helped Naipaul to find himself.

REFERENCES

1. Naipaul, Interview with Francis Wyndham, *Sunday Times*, 10 Sep. 1968: 24.
2. Linda A. Newson, *Aboriginal and Spanish Colonial Trinidad: A Study in Culture Contact* (London: Academic Press, 1976), 77.
3. Linda Newson, *Aboriginal and Spanish Colonial Trinidad*, 182.
4. Elbaki Hermassi, *The Third World Reassessed*, 157.
5. Naipaul, *Passage*, 44.
6. Naipaul, *Street*, 216.
7. Bibhu Padhi, "Naipaul on Naipaul and the Novel," *Modern Fiction Studies*, 30.3 (1984), 495.
8. Naipaul, *Street*, 163.
9. Seepersad Naipaul, *The Adventures of Gurudava and other Short Stories* (London: Andre Duetsch, 1976).
10. Francis Wyndham, *The London Magazine*, Sep. 1959: 78-79.
11. Naipaul, *Passage*, 82.
12. *Ibid.*, 83.
13. Naipaul, *Street*, 79.
14. *Ibid.*, 17.
15. Naipaul, *Passage*, 75.
16. Eric Williams, *History of the People of Trinidad and Tobago*, 39.
17. Naipaul, *Street*, 12.
18. *Ibid.*, 190.

19. Naipaul, *Street*, 23.
20. *Ibid.*, 27.
21. *Ibid.*, 111.
22. *Ibid.*, 68.
23. *Ibid.*, 68.
24. *Ibid.*, 69.
25. *Ibid.*, 115.
26. *Ibid.*, 115.
27. *Ibid.*, 34.
28. *Ibid.*, 34.
29. *Ibid.*, 17.
30. *Ibid.*, 18.
31. *Ibid.*, 71.
32. *Ibid.*, 188.
33. *Ibid.*, 15.
34. *Ibid.*, 185.
35. *Ibid.*, 185.
36. *Ibid.*, 216.
37. Madhusudana Rao, *Contrary Awareness*, 31.
38. Naipaul, *House*, 17.
39. *Ibid.*, 17.
40. *Ibid.*, 32.
41. *Ibid.*, 15.
42. *Ibid.*, 15.
43. *Ibid.*, 590.
44. *Ibid.*, 40.
45. *Ibid.*, 51.
46. *Ibid.*, 51.
47. *Ibid.*, 52.
48. *Ibid.*, 58.
49. *Ibid.*, 65.
50. *Ibid.*, 67.
51. *Ibid.*, 78-79.
52. *Ibid.*, 79.
53. *Ibid.*, 79.
54. *Ibid.*, 79.
55. Kenneth Ramchand, *The West Indian Novel and its Background* (London: Faber and Faber, 1970), 204.
56. Maureen Warner-Lewis, "Cultural Confrontation, Disintegration and

Syncretism in *A House for Mr. Biswas.*" *Critical perspectives on V.S. Naipaul*, 98.

57. Maureen Warner-Lewis, "Cultural Confrontation," *Critical Perspectives*, 98.
58. Naipaul, *Passage*, 60.
59. Naipaul, *House*, 46.
60. *Ibid.*, 46.
61. *Ibid.*, 97.
62. *Ibid.*, 107.
63. Gordon Rohlehr, "The Ironic approach," *Critical Perspectives*, 189.
64. Naipaul, *House*, 131.
65. *Ibid.*, 125.
66. *Ibid.*, 147.
67. *Ibid.*, 390.
68. *Ibid.*, 188.
69. *Ibid.*, 190.
70. *Ibid.*, 279.
71. *Ibid.*, 303.
72. *Ibid.*, 230.
73. *Ibid.*, 231.
74. *Ibid.*, 231.
75. *Ibid.*, 332.
76. *Ibid.*, 337.
77. *Ibid.*, 340.
78. *Ibid.*, 407-8.
79. *Ibid.*, 402.
80. *Ibid.*, 412.
81. *Ibid.*, 436.
82. *Ibid.*, 424.
83. *Ibid.*, 424.
84. *Ibid.*, 438.
85. *Ibid.*, 585.
86. *Ibid.*, 551.
87. *Ibid.*, 12.
88. *Ibid.*, 580.
89. Madhusudana Rao, *Contrary Awareness*, 99.
90. Naipaul, *House*, 572.
91. *Ibid.*, 589.
92. Landeg White, *V.S. Naipaul: A Critical Introduction*, 88.

93. Gordon Rohlehr, "The Ironic Approach," *Critical Perspectives*, 190.
94. Francis Wyndham, "V.S. Naipaul," *Listener*, 7 Oct., 1971: 462.
95. Naipaul, *House*, 97.
96. Charles Michener, "The Dark Visions of V.S. Naipaul," *Newsweek*, 16 Nov. 1981, 108.
97. Madhusudana Rao, *Contrary Awareness*, 97.
98. Gordon Rohlehr, "The Ironic Approach," *Critical Perspectives*, 191.
99. Naipaul, *Return*, 211.

4

The Postcolonial Society and The Paradox of Freedom in *The Mimic Men*, *A Flag on The Island* and *In a Free State*

The empires of our time were shortlived, but they have altered the world for ever; their passing away is their least significant feature.[1]

—V.S. Naipaul

In his early novels, Naipaul was mainly engaged in reconstructing his personal experiences in the fictional form in an attempt to come to terms with his own displacement. With the writing of *House* the problems had been partly resolved. For though Naipaul still could not "lay claim" to his portion of the earth, as such, he had at least established his home identity. *House* marks the culmination of the first phase of Naipaul's career wherein he was, as he himself says, simply recording his reactions to the world and had not come to any conclusions about it.[2] It is only in the next phase, with *Passage* that a conscious attempt to analyse his reactions is made for the first time. Writing *House* had been "like a career" for Naipaul, but it had left him feeling artistically enervated. He had begun to realize, too, that "it wasn't easy for the exotic writer to get his work accepted as being more than something exotic."[3] It was in part to rid himself of the fear of artistic sterility that had set upon him after the completion of *House* and in part his desire to be something more than a regional writer, that led him to write *Mr. Stone*, in which he deals with exclusively English characters in an exclusively English setting. This novel may be regarded as a transitional work that helped him to cut across regional boundaries and secure a place for himself among the writers of the mainstream. However, since *Mr. Stone* does not demonstrate an immediate and obvious concern with Third World Societies, it remains outside the purview of the present study.

Naipaul is a writer who has always felt physical distance from his subject necessary for an objective presentation of his material. Just as his first four novels had been written in London, in order to write about England he felt the need to refresh himself by travel.[4] Travel indeed proved to be an important stimulus for the further development of his art. For, it not only helped Naipaul to overcome his uncertainties but also enabled him to find his vision. This is clearly evident from what Naipaul says in *Centre*:

> To travel was glamorous. But travel also made unsuspected demands on me as a man and a writer, and perhaps for that reason it soon became a necessary stimulus for me. It broadened my world view; it showed me a changing world and took me out of my own colonial shell; it became the substitute for the mature social experience—the deepening knowledge of a society—which my background and the nature of my life denied me. My uncertainty about my role withered; a role was not necessary. I recognized my own instincts as a traveller, and was content to be myself, to be what I had always been, a looker. And I learned to look in my own way.[5]

Travel, thus, broadened his perspective and made it possible for him to view his personal emptiness and homelessness against the wider context of the larger world. This explains the marked shift in emphasis from the earlier preoccupations which happened to be of a rather personal nature, to the broader, more general themes that emerge in the works belonging to the second phase.

In addition to the broadening of vision, there is an essential difference in approach that draws a clear line between the novels of the two phases. The difference lies in the fact that the insights gained by Naipaul in the course of his travels greatly modified his notions about art and artistic responsibility. He came to realise that creative novels of the kind he had written in the early phase of his career, fulfilled only part of the writer's commitment—his commitment to art—and left the larger commitment to his society unfulfilled. Such novels made sense only within the framework of an ordered society where "after a disturbance there is calm, and all crises fall back into that great underlying calm."[6] However, for people living in a "disordered and fast changing world," novels of the purely imaginative nature far removed from the social reality could hold no meaning. Naipaul came to believe that writers addressing such societies have a greater purpose to serve than the mere fulfilment of the aesthetic function. It is Naipaul's conviction that people living in a disordered and fast changing world need help in "grasping it, understanding [and] controlling it,"[7] and this is the greater purpose a writer has to serve. In one of his articles entitled "The Documentary Heresy," Naipaul makes his conception of the novelist's duty very clear when he says: "The artist who, for political or humanitarian reasons, seeks only to record abandons half his responsibility. He becomes a participant; he becomes anonymous. He does not impose a vision on the world."[8] Andrew Gurr, a critic discussing Naipaul's works, reads these statements of Naipaul's as a rejection of *House* and what he was doing in his first four novels.[9] However, though Naipaul was mainly fulfilling the recording function of an artist in those novels, it was directed towards a specific end. By recording his ancestry he was trying to impose an order on his disordered life and retrieve his identity from a jumbled past. Trying to capture a sense of the past, one's cultural history, one's home, though backward looking, as Andrew Gurr points out, is still very relevant and crucial to those trapped in the colonial situation. But we agree with the critic that in the context of the postcolonial societies "such a function lacks the sense of urgency which the new political present insists on."[10]

Significantly, therefore, Naipaul's writings in the post-independence period tends to be serious and reflective. In his non-fiction, Naipaul examines postcolonial societies and the conclusions he arrives at therein find a restatement in the novels. In the novels written in the post-independence period, Naipaul surfaces as a novelist of post-imperial crisis. His despair is effectively conveyed in the grim and humourless tone of the novels. Naipaul's vision of the world, henceforth, becomes progressively bleak and the tone, accordingly, becomes more and more grim. Thus, *Mimic Men, A Flag on the Island* and *In a Free State* set the tone for the forthcoming novels. All the three works of fiction portray newly independent colonies. *Mimic* is set in a fictional Caribbean island, while *State* is much wider in scope. The title story takes us to a newly independent African country in a state of revolution. Two of the three stories, though set outside the Third World, feature Indians and relate in one way or another to being "in a free state."

The themes of alienation, homelessness and mimicry still preoccupy Naipaul, but the perspective has changed. They are now viewed as a universal condition of the modern world afflicting both colonized and colonizers alike. Besides the familiar themes that still haunt Naipaul's pen, there are themes that appear for the first time—the broader postcolonial themes of power and freedom and neocolonialism.

In an interview with Ronald Bryden in 1973, Naipaul observes: "All my work is really one. I'm really writing one big book."[11] In the preceding chapters we saw the interrelation between the first four novels. The interrelation and continuity of themes between *Mimic* and the preceding novels becomes immediately apparent. For, while the displaced colonials of the earlier novels cherished England as the land of opportunities and escape to England meant an escape from all miseries, in *Mimic* however, London is exposed for what it is—a mirage, a mere illusion—and the "promised land" turns out to be equally fraudulent. Thematic continuity is further maintained through a much more comprehensive treatment of the concept of identity. For, with political independence another dimension has been added making Ralph Singh's search for an identity in *Mimic*, a more complex affair as he has to locate himself within the new socio-political framework.

Before proceeding further it would be relevant to establish the connection between the narrator protagonist of *Mimic* and Naipaul, the author. While in the preceding novels Naipaul had maintained his separateness from his characters through the use of irony, in *Mimic*, however, Naipaul makes no attempt to maintain his separate identity. At no point in the novel do we witness Singh becoming the target of Naipaul's irony. In *Masseur* there was the narrator's version which contradicted Ganesh's version to guide our responses. Similarly, in *Street* we had the dichotomy of the dual perspective of the narrator as a boy and as an adult to highlight the ironies. The absence of such manipulations in *Mimic* leads one to conclude that Singh and Naipaul are in fact one. We are too familiar with Naipaul's artistic expertise to consider it a lapse on his part. The merging of identities is further underscored by the fact that many of Naipaul's attitudes and tastes are transferred onto Singh. There are instances in the novel where Singh sounds very much like Naipaul. In *Area* Naipaul expressing his disillusionment with London says: "I came to London. It had become the centre of my world and I had worked hard to come to it. And I was lost. London was not the centre of my world." He then goes on to say: "In the big city I was confined to a smaller world than I had ever known."[12] Singh too had considered London to be the centre of his world and he too expresses his disillusionment in a similar way. The idea of constriction is expressed almost exactly by Singh when he says: "My life has never been more physically limited than it has been during these last three years."[13] Again, Singh too shares Naipaul's admiration for rich people. In an interview with Nigel Bingham in 1972 Naipaul says: "For a long, long time I used to worship people with money...."[14] In *Mimic* we find Singh showing the same admiration. Referring to his Jewish landlord he says: "And for Mr. Shylock, the recipient each week of fifteen times three guineas, the possessor of a mistress and of suits made of cloth so fine I felt I could eat it, I had nothing but admiration."[15] Even Sandra, Singh's English wife, is modelled on Laraine, an American girl, whom Naipaul met during his pilgrimage to Amarnath. Like her, Sandra is lean and her skin has the same Quality of graining. Singh is thus representative of Naipaul, and his reconciliation to his lot signifies Naipaul's own reconciliation to his displacement.

At this point it would be useful to consider an important outcome of Naipaul's travels—the focus on landscape. In the first three novels written prior to his travels hardly any attention is paid to the landscape as such. It is only from *House* onwards that a conscious interest in the landscape first becomes evident. Naipaul turns his attention to the landscape not for its own sake, but in search of a native historical tradition. In the case of *House* the landscape emerges as a crucial element, but one tied to personal rather than more inclusive national histories.[16] In *Mimic* however, the landscape is scanned more for the national history that it carries and which is now recognized as a necessary condition for establishing a more stable identity. It is precisely because Singh, the protagonist in *Mimic*, is unable to relate himself to his immediate landscape but fantasizes about an ideal landscape, that a stable identity eludes him. Whereas, others like the Deschampsneufs are able to experience a sense of place only because they are receptive to the landscape and identify with it. Deschampsneufs tells Singh that one's birth place is one's ultimate source of identity:

> ...oh, yes, we all want to get away and so on. But where you are born is a funny thing. My great-grandfather and even my grandfather, they always talked about going back for good. But they came back. You know, you are born in a place and you grow up there. You get to know the trees and the plants. You will never know any other trees and plants like that.... Where you born, man, you born. And this island is a paradise, you will discover.[17]

But of course, Mr. Deschampneufs is able to say so from the "security of his aristocracy." The Deschampneufs enjoy a privileged position in the island being one of the old French families and the descendents of slave-owners. But Singh, being "the late intruder" cannot link himself to the landscape or the people in the same way that the Deschampneufs can. He, therefore, supplants the real landscape with imaginary ones. Till the end he never really finds his landscape. Even when he returns to Isabella, after his disillusionment with London, his opinion about Isabella has not altered. Though from on board the ship it appears to be "pure" and "fresh," Singh knows the reality: "And I knew it to be, horribly, man made; to be exhausted, fraudulent, cruel and, above all, not mine."[18] This idea about the artificial nature of the landscape appears as a refrain in all Naipaul's works from *Mimic* onwards. The landscape in "A Flag on the Island," the title story of *Flag*, turns out to be engineered by the Americans and the resort in the title story of *State* happens to be a creation of the colonizers, "who thought, they had come to Africa to stay, and looked in a resort for a version of the things of home: a park, a pier, a waterside promenade."[19] In *State* all the characters portrayed are far removed from the landscape of their nativity. Though these characters become aware of the landscape, they fail to get a sense of place because they realize that it can never be their's in the real sense.

The treatment of the landscape in the subsequent novels, *Guerrillas* and *Bend* mirror Naipaul's own bleak vision of the world. There is no positive outcome of Naipaul's search either for an order or a native historical tradition in the landscape and the search is finally abandoned in *Bend* in which all that Naipaul is able to see is an inhospitable "bush" history which yields no foundation for a society.

Mimic is presented to us in the form of a fictional autobiography in which Singh, a political exile in London, meditates on the fragments which form his life. There is much in his wrecked life to reckon with: an uneasy childhood, a painful youth, a broken marriage and an abortive political career. Living alone in a suburban London hotel room, Singh, drawing on his memory writes his memories in order to salvage what he can from his shipwrecked life. Commenting about the narrative technique of the novel, William Walsh observes that it is "dissolving and non-linear in correspondence with the instrument of self-examination."[20] The self-examination Singh subjects himself to, raises his memoirs from the level of a personal self-confessional report to that of a reliable document elucidating on the problems of the emergent nations of the Third World.

Singh's memoirs come to us in three parts. In the first part Singh records his disillusionment with London, his marriage with Sandra, an English girl, their return to Isabella followed by Singh's rise in business and finally the breakdown of his marriage. In the second part Singh reverts back to his childhood while in the final section of the novel he gives an account of his political career.

Singh comes to London, full of hopes, thinking it to be

the centre of his world, where he is at last to find fulfilment. Singh confesses that while at Isabella, the island of his birth, he had been painfully aware of his ambiguous New World background: "To be descended from generations of idlers and failures, an unbroken line of the unimaginative, unenterprising and oppressed, had always seemed to me to be a cause for deep, silent shame."[21] Singh's frank account of his childhood reveals the materialistic nature of the society of Isabella, where it is considered a disgrace to be poor. Singh's father is a poor school teacher and so Singh prefers to lay claim to his mother's family only because they are among the richest in the island. In Isabella, even children live dual lives and are borne-down by secrets. Singh's childhood is burdened with secrets he longs to be rid of. The duality is introduced into their lives because in Isabella, as in any colonial society, the school and the home remain two separate hemispheres.

In school every boy lived with a fantasy of his own and concealed the real life of the home. That is why, Hok, one of Singh's classmates ignores his mother on one occasion when he is with his classmates. When this is reported to the teacher he is outraged and makes Hok go back and wish her. Hok breaks down into tears because he feels exposed and Singh provides the reasons: "It wasn't only that the mother was black and of the people, though that was a point; it was that he had been expelled from that private hemisphere of fantasy where lay his true life."[22] The pressure that a colonial society exerts on the psyche of even small boys is expressed through the episode. It is clear from what Singh says that it is the colonial education that leads them to deny the reality around them:

> Anything that touched on everyday life excited laughter when it was mentioned in a classroom: the name of a street, the name of street-corner foods. The laughter denied our knowledge of these things to which after the hours of school we were to return. We denied the landscape and the people we could see out of open doors and windows, we who took apples to the teacher and wrote essays about visits to temperate farms. Whether

> we dissected a hibiscus flower or recited the names of Isabellan birds, school remained a private hemisphere.[23]

Singh too, fashions his own fantasies in which he imagines that he is a shipwrecked chieftain on an unknown shore, "awaiting rescue, awaiting the arrival of ships of curious shape to take him back to mountains."[24] Eden, Singh's classmate has his own dreams of a "remote land where he, the solitary Negro among an alien pretty people, ruled as a sort of sexual king."[25] Singh tries out other ways of overcoming his sense of inadequacy. For instance, he starts calling himself "Ralph" rejecting even his real name which is "Ranjit," as if a change of name would make him a different person. This becomes one of his "heavy secrets" and keeps him in a constant fear of discovery at home. Such instances provide an adequate commentary on the society which drives even children to such acts of deception. We are reminded once again that the sense of one's reality lying elsewhere is a typical malady of the colonized people. We realize too, that the only alternative left to colonials who deny their reality is mimicry.

Singh's conclusions about Isabella are strikingly similar to those arrived at by Naipaul in *Passage*. In Singh's words: "To be born on an island like Isabella, an obscure New World transplantation, second-hand and barbarous, was to be born to disorder."[26] He thus resolves to leave Isabella and make a fresh start in London. However, because of his father's religio-political movement his plans of escape gets delayed and the connection he had tried to suppress only gets further strengthened. Later on, it becomes the pretext on which his own political career commences.

The political agitation started by Singh's father begins quite abruptly. One afternoon, Singh's father fails to return home from work and the next thing they know is that he has become "a preacher, a leader with a growing frenzied following."[27] In a gesture of protest Singh's father leads the distressed and disaffected to the hills in order to settle them on crown land. The striking dock workers also join him. Singh's father becomes "Gurudeva." People in Isabella feel that they have at last "caught up with the other disturbed territories in the region."[28] However, after creating a sensation, the movement dies out having neither philosophy nor a cause to keep it sustained. Singh, who has to face embarrassments in school because of his father's political movement feels betrayed. By this time, though, the insularity of the school has been broken. In spite of his indifference towards his father, Singh finds it difficult to remain totally detached from the movement because the role of "the son of a leader suddenly found" is thrust upon him. Nevertheless, Singh's attitude towards the whole affair remains ambivalent. As he himself confesses: "With some boys I was as detached as before about my father's movement, though their criticism still pained me. And then I could not reject the conspiratorial devotion of the others."[29] At the same time Singh feels repulsed by the devotion offered to him by Browne and the others, who have begun to look upon him as their Messiah's son.

The killing of Tamango, the favorite racehorse for the Malay Cup which marks the culmination of Singh's father's movement, horrifies Singh. What horrifies Singh is not just the killing, but the fact that it is done in the ritualistic manner of the "Asvamedha" the ancient horse sacrifice, which in Singh's imagination is "a thing of beauty, speaking of the youth of the world, of untrodden forests and unsullied streams, of horses and warrior-youths in morning light...."[30] When even his private world of fantasy is intruded into and rendered obscene, Singh experiences an urgent need for withdrawal. An acute existential fear grips Singh when, while on a beach holiday, he witnesses a drowning accident. This is his first lesson about the "weakness of the flesh." A deep fear of extinction haunts him. Even when he is in his grandfather's solid and strong house, he begins to jump on the floor and lean against the walls to test their strength. On one occasion while he is watching the afternoon show, it suddenly begins to rain heavily. He runs home in panic but is relieved to find his house safe. Paradoxically however, he also feels disappointed and he explains that it is "the disappointment of someone who had been denied the chance of making a fresh start, alone."[31] About this time an incestuous relationship develops between Singh and Sally, his cousin. His grandfather's house had been a refuge for Singh while his grandfather lived. With his Grandfather's death however, the house begins to be invaded by Cecil's friends with whom Singh finds himself ill at ease. He now seeks refuge in the clandestine relationship with Sally. It is this relationship that defines all his other relationships with women. For, in every other relationship he experiences either triumph or humiliation but never the "mutual acceptance" found in the first. In this as well as in Eden's dream of ruling as a sort of sexual king, we witness the extent to which colonialism has corrupted even the most apolitical of all relationships—the relation between the sexes. This testifies that in the colonial ethos every relationship is reduced to the colonial binary of Domination and Subordination. Men like Singh are the products of colonialism, damaged both at the psychological and spiritual levels.

Singh's long-awaited release from Isabella finally comes when he is accepted by the London School. On coming to London he takes a room in a boarding house owned by a Jew. His first experience of Snow turns bitter when he goes into the attic of the boarding house to get a better view of the snow fall, but gets a peep into his late landlord's secret life of pleasure. He feels all the magic of the city go away with this exposure of the forlorness of the city and the people who live in it. In London, Singh experiences a deeper fragmentation and instead of the flowering of personality, he encounters a greater confusion. There is the same sense of isolation and absence, of correlation between the people and the landscape:

> Those of us who came to it lost some of our solidity; we were trapped into fixed, flat postures. And, in this growing dissociation between ourselves and the city in which we walked, scores of separate meetings, not Linked even by ourselves, who became nothing more than perceivers: Everyone reduced, reciprocally, to a succession of such meetings, so that first experience and then the personality divided bewilderingly into compartments. Each person concealed his own darkness.[32]

Throughout the novel, Naipaul conveys the idea that identity is a feeble entity for colonials. Singh first gets this insight when his grandfather is insulted by some labourers. Though they are just labourers, their insult deeply affects Singh's grandfather and Singh gets his first political lesson: "A man was only what he saw of himself in others...."[33] In London,

Singh seeks reassurance in Lieni's eyes and gets into the role of the extravagant colonial that she fashions for him. To rid himself of his inner emptiness he begins to visit brothels. He is on the verge of a mental breakdown when Sandra, whom he has known for some time, leads him to propose to her. Singh is attracted by the aura of good luck about her as well as her sense of sureness and precision which he himself lacks. In reality however, Sandra's position is no better than Singh's. Though she belongs to the metropolis, she too is a drifter and like Singh has rejected her family. At the moment she asks Singh to marry her, she is just about as uncertain about her future because having failed a qualifying examination, the route of escape through education is no longer available to her.

Soon after marriage Singh and Sandra leave for Isabella, but at the port itself Singh's mother creates an embarrassing scene by refusing to accept Sandra and instead of going home, they go to a hotel. Singh finds the post-war Isabella greatly changed. It no longer seems mean and constricting. Singh and Sandra attach themselves to a "neutral, fluid group" of young men who have studied abroad and have "expatriate and fantastically cosmopolitan wives or girl friends."[34] In this society, Singh experiences a solidity, feeling for the first time that his character is not "what others took it to be, but something personal and ordained."[35] Sandra too feels avid and appreciative. Singh makes a fortune by developing the land his grandfather has left him. However, the island life soon begins to tire Sandra and she withdraws into her shell. Something also goes wrong between the couple and they drift away from each other. Singh relapses into his old habit and starts seeking pleasure in affairs outside marriage. As Singh later reflects it was the barrenness of their relationship which promised no growth, that led to the rift between them. He nevertheless, holds himself responsible for not doing anything to save the marriage. He realizes that he had let Sandra sink into despair, when even a mere physical demonstration of anger could have revived the relationship.

In her own despair, Sandra starts hurting the racial susceptibilities of people for, every thing in the island has begun to seem inferior to her. In the meanwhile, the construction of Singh's house gets completed, but it has ceased to have any meaning for either of them. The house-warming party ends in unpleasantness when the guests suddenly get into a destructive mood and start breaking things. The party underscores the deep disorder that forms the reality of societies like Isabella. Singh leaves the party in a fit of rage and by the time he returns the guests have all left. He silently retires to his room as by this time he and Sandra have started living in separate rooms, and no longer share a relationship where consolation can be sought or given. After the house-warming party the rift between them widens. Sandra takes the ultimate step by leaving the island. She leaves behind a note for Singh in which she writes: "The Niger is a tributary of that Seine."[36] This highlights the racial difference between them.

Soon after Sandra's departure, Singh led on by Browne, his former school friend, embarks on his political career. Browne, who is now the editor of "The Socialist" plans to celebrate the anniversary of the dock worker's exodus from the city as the first gesture towards independence and urges Singh to contribute the main article about his father. The article is written and with the publication of the anniversary issue of the new-look socialist, their political movement gets launched. They win the elections and Browne becomes the Prime Minister while Singh is made a Cabinet Minister. It is only on coming to power that Singh comes to realize the futility inherent to the New World politician's situation. Singh's failure to bring about the nationalization of the sugar estates provokes race riots and he is forced to make his escape to London. It is only when he begins writing his memoirs that Singh reflects on his political career and comes to understand the fraudulence of power in the emergent nations of the Third World which lack order. The political career of the colonial politician finds an apt portrayal in the following passage:

> The career of a colonial politician is short and ends brutally. We lack order. Above all, we lack power, and we do not understand that we lack power. We mistake words and the acclamation of words for power; as soon as our bluff is called we are lost. Politics for us are a do-or-die, once-for-all charge. Once we are committed we

> fight more than political battles; we often fight quite literally for our lives. Our transitional or makeshift societies do no cushion us. There are no universities or City houses to refresh us and absorb us after the heat of battle. For those who lose, and nearly everyone in the end loses, there is only one course: flight. Flight to the greater disorder, the final emptiness: London and the home counties.[37]

Singh makes it clear that his political career is not unusual, but a typical example of the career of colonial politicians. What he is giving account of has happened in "twenty places, twenty countries islands, colonies, territories...." What is required by government of such countries is sound policy, but Singh's government had offered only drama. They had gone no further than a statement of distress. Having won the elections through mob-power, they had thought the mob to be the source of all power. It was only later that they came to realize that in the emergent countries like theirs the mob "without skills, was unproductive, offered nothing, and was in the end without power."[38] Without trade unions, organized capital and a force of nationalism their power was useless. Under such circumstances even a sincere politician can do nothing. A politician, according to Singh is "a man lifted out of himself."[39] Consequently, he has to view everything as an issue. This is the reason why Singh's party is unable to fulfil the promises made before the elections. Without knowing the reality, they had included the expulsion of the white expatriates in their agenda. It was only after coming into power that they realized the economic impossibility of such a proposition. They were also incapable of doing without the technical expertise of the expatriates. This is the inevitable fate of Third World nations which lack local expertise and continue to depend on the mother country for ideas, technologies and financial aid. Through Singh, Naipaul draws attention to the neocolonialism to which the emergent nations fall victim because of their dependence on outside power. The economy thus suffers due to the manipulations of forcign investors. Industrialization in such countries is bound to end up as no more than a "process of filling imported tubes and tins with various imported substances."[40] Political independence is nothing more than a mockery.

The Third World's penchant for foreign goods also comes under criticism. This aspect is reflected in the failure of the only purely local endeavour of canning local fruit. Singh observes: "It hadn't occurred to anyone concerned to find out whether local people wanted local fruit tinned...."[41] In the ultimate analysis, the crux of the problem is identified in the nature of the society itself:

> But on power and the consolidation of passing power we wasted our energies, until the bigger truth came: that in a society like ours, fragmented, inorganic, no link between man and the landscape, a society not held together by common interests, there was no true internal source of power, and that no power was real which did not come from outside.[42]

What exists instead of society is only a kind of "controlled chaos." Movements like the one carried out by Singh's father might not have had philosophy or a cause but at least there had been one positive outcome: It had shocked people out of their delusions by generating disorder in the ostensible order. What the post-independence politicians did was just antithetical. By the outwards semblance of order that they offered, they deluded people into believing that there was order. By hiring English secretaries the ministers of the post-independence period offered their people "the spectacle of the black man served by the white...."[43] This was the revolution they claimed to have created.

In spite of all the images of Shipwreck, *Mimic* is one of the most optimistic of Naipaul's later novels. At the end of the novel, Singh can still claim that he has "cleared the decks" and prepared himself for fresh action. He is even confident that it will be the action of a "free man." Through the act of writing his memoirs, Singh has come to understand and accept the finality of his displacement and is now well-equipped to begin afresh.

While *Mimic* examines the paradox of power in relation to the postcolonial politicians, *Flag* illustrates the confusion that prevails in the postcolonial society after the coming of independence. *Flag* is a collection of short stories. However, the title story is closer in form to the novella than to the short story or even the long short story. Referring to the title story, "A Flag on the Island," Madhusudana Rao observes: "'A Flag on the Island' is something more than a long short story; it tends to be a novella with a tensely regulated movement of action, culminating in a symbolic finish."[44] "A Flag on the Island" is a commissioned work written for an American film company.

The writing of *Flag* and *Mimic* overlap each other and there is a close affinity in the theme and structure of the two works. Both works focus on the unreality of postcolonial societies that have become newly independent and both have the same tripartite structure. However, there are some basic differences that place the two works on different planes. *Flag* provides a panoramic view of the society as a whole but *Mimic* focuses more on the development of the individual personality. More importantly, the first person narrator-protagonist in *Flag*, being an American is an outsider, whereas in *Mimic* he is an East-Indian and belongs to the society he describes. Hence, the process by which Singh in *Mimic* arrives at his assessment is a much more complex one compared to Frankie, who as an outsider can view things objectively. It is this distance from the experience that places the two works on different planes. Frankie's perspective is essentially that of the "other" and though he carries the burden of a guilt-complex, he, unlike Singh has a place to return to.

In the first part of the novella, Frankie, the narrator-protagonist finds himself once again on the Caribbean island (where he had been stationed as a soldier at the American base during the Second World War) when his ship is forced to dock because of a threatened hurricane. As Frankie goes into the island, he sees that though the island now has a flag of its own, its people have if anything, become even more unreal than before because they now strive to live up to the tourist's image of themselves. Political independence has not released them from their psychological bondage to the colonizer's culture and they continue to live dual lives. This is evident in the taxi driver's nostalgia for the flag of the colonial days. He tells Frankie: "...but I prefer the old Union

Jack. It look like a real flag. This look like something they make up you know, like foreign money?"[45]

The second part of the novella is a flashback, which carries us back to the time when Frankie was a soldier at the American base in the island and had first become acquainted with, Henry, Selma, Blackwhite and Priest. Henry used to run a brothel in the name of a cultural centre. It was here that he had first met Selma, whose craze for "nice modern things"[46] had brought her there. Frankie had bought a house in the street and they had started living together casually. Blackwhite Ma-Ho and Priest are also residents of the street. Blackwhite calls himself the principal of a premier commercial college and is also a struggling story-writer, whose love stories about "lords and ladies" relate in no way to the reality of his life. Ma-Ho, is a Chinese, who runs a grocery in the street. He considers himself a temporary resident in the street and has plans of going back to China. Priest is another contradictory character, who first frightens people with his sermons about death and then sells them insurance. Then there is Mano who joins walking races but always ends up running. Through Frankie's help Mano finally wins the race but instead of rejoicing he commits suicide and it becomes known that Mano had actually wanted to be a runner. This episode serves as a comment on the negative outcome of the American interference. The economic boom created by the American presence also has a corrupting effect on the people. Mr. Lambert, the bookbinder had a contented life in his small wooden house but his life becomes miserable when he starts earning twenty dollars a day by hiring out the truck Frankie has stolen for him from the base. His wife gets the old house dismantled and has a concrete house constructed in its place. She starts ill-treating Mr. Lambert and in the end even denies him entry in the house. Selma chides Frankie for his interference in other people's lives: "I don't think you should go around interfering any more in other people's lives. People don't really want what you think they want."[47]

Reminiscing about the time when the island had been flagless, Frankie recalls that the island was then "a city of ridiculous affirmations." Blackwhite's coloured portrait of Haile Selassie in his front room and the photograph of Chiang Kai-

Shek, that Ma-Ho kept concealed between his Chinese calendars were ridiculous affirmations that denied the existence of the island. Blackwhite and Ma-Ho deluded themselves by thinking that they had places to return to when the war ended. With independence, however, the island has a claim to existence and the flag brings the message of its affirmation. Now, there is no escape for people like Blackwhite and Ma-Ho, who cherished dreams of another world. Just before independence comes to the island, Ma-Ho dies all of a sudden and his family gets a lot of insurance money. Till then Ma-Ho's family had maintained their insularity by keeping to themselves:

> His children remained distinctive, and separate from the life of the street: a small neat crocodile, each child armed with neat bags and neat pencil boxes, going coolly off to school in the morning and returning just as coolly in the afternoon, as though nothing had touched them during the whole day, or caused them to be sullied. In the morning the back door of his shop opened to let out these children; in the afternoon the back door opened to swallow them in again; and nothing more was heard from them; and nothing more was seen of them.[48]

With Ma-Ho's death this insularity is broken:

> Ma-Ho went, and with him there also went the Chinese emblems in his shop. No longer the neat crocodile left and entered the back door of the shop; and from being people who kept themselves to themselves, who gave the impression of being only temporary residents on the island, always packed for departure, Ma-Ho's family came out. The girls began to ride bicycles. The insurance money was good. The boys began to play cricket on the pavement. And Mrs. Ma-Ho, who had never spoken a word of English, revealed that she could speak the language.[49]

Blackwhite not only abandons the idea of going back but thinks of giving up writing in the English language and championing the cause of the native language. He tells Frankie:

> What we want is our own language. I intend to write in our own language. You know this patios we have. Not English, not French, but something we have made up.

> This is our own. You were right. Damn those lords and ladies. Damn Jane Austen. This is ours. This is what we have to work with....[50]

Blackwhite's enthusiasm, however, does not go beyond the statement and ends with only an additional line on the board outside his house—PATIOS TAUGHT HERE. He continues to write in English what his English patrons want him to write, crushing the Third World consciousness before it has evolved. When the war is over, it is only Frankie and his fellow Americans who leave the island. There is one positive outcome of Frankie's interference in Blackwhite's case. It is Frankie who first tells Blackwhite that he should write about the life around him instead of weaving romances around lords and ladies. Blackwhite follows his advice and achieves success.

The final part of the novella brings us back to the present and takes up the story from the point at which the first part had stopped. Frankie sets foot on the island a second time and notices that the island has changed. He first goes in search of his house but finds only a vacant plot where his house had stood. When he meets Selma she tells him that she has sold the house to a foundation and got a nicer, more modern house in a better locality. Selma's new house mimicks the modernistic style that has caught on in the island:

> ...Selma's house was in the modernistic style of the island. Lawn, garden, a swimming pool shaped like a tear-drop. The roof of the veranda was supported on sloping lights of tubular metal. The ceiling was in varnished pitchpine. The furnishings were equally contemporary. Little bits of driftwood; electric lights pretending to be oil lamps; irregularly shaped tables whose tops were sections of tree trunks complete with bark....[51]

Frankie is struck by the change that has come over the island and its people. Henry's cultural centre is no longer a place where people can walk in casually. It is now a formal joint where only people wearing ties are allowed in. Henry is himself formally dressed in a suit. Blackwhite now calls himself H.J.B. White and Priest, now Gary priestland has become a TV personality. The change, we see, has taken place at a superficial level only. There is no inner transformation in the people to match the external changes that are so glaringly visible. Frankie notices that American money and influence still defines the people's tastes as the islanders strive to live up to the image that the tourist brochures have created for them. In the name of promoting native culture, the Americans provide sponsorship only to those local artists who cater to their requirements. Once an artist stops being useful to them he is coolly dropped for another more suppliant one. Blackwhite has patrons running after him so long as he writes inter-racial love stories but when he tries to be innovative by writing about a black man falling in love with a black woman, he is immediately dropped for his "crazy ideas."[52]

Towards the end of the novel, the people, if only momentarily drop their pretences when they come to know that their island is going to be destroyed by the hurricane. The news sends a wave of relief, and there is a lot of rejoicing among the people who rejoice at the prospect of being released once and for all from the inauthentic kind of lives that they all are forced to live. The news releases them from their public roles and makes them private individuals once again. However, even this chance of escape ends in disappointment as the hurricane is averted and some other island is destroyed. Once again the islanders have to accommodate themselves to their fate and in the end it is only Frankie and the other tourists who leave the island.

The themes of mimicry and inferiority of postcolonial societies run like a refrain through all Naipaul's works. The carnival episode in *Flag* foregrounds the mimicking tendency of postcolonial societies. On the first day of the carnival, Blackwhite goes dressed in a fantastically braided uniform as "MacArthur, promising to return,"[53] and on the second evening he poses as Shakespeare. The street on those two evenings are "full of great figures—Napoleon, Julius Caesar, Richard the Lion Heart...."[54] In all Naipaul's works, inferiority of postcolonial societies remains a fixed idea. Naipaul holds the colonial past of these societies responsible for their deficiencies. People living in these societies cannot rise above their mediocrity. We find a reiteration of this idea in *Flag* too when Blackwhite tells Frankie that had Churchill been born on the island, even he would have ended up "importing sewing machines and exporting cocoa."[55] Naipaul makes it clear that the society plays a major role in moulding an individual's potentialities by providing avenues for developing them. Singh in *Mimic* learns the lesson the hard way. He realizes that unskilled mob cannot be the source of real power.

In his next work, *State,* Naipaul probes into the paradoxical nature of freedom which instead of liberating the colonial subjects only makes them the "...casualities of that freedom."[56]

As Naipaul's art matures an increasing importance is given to ideas and Naipaul becomes more concerned with thought, meaning and philosophy. Simultaneously, style and structure lose importance. This is apparent from what Naipaul himself says on the subject:

> As you grow older you begin to write more profoundly; you are thinking less of the way the words lie on the paper, and more of the meanings, the timing, the emphasis—not thinking of style or language at all; just the effect.... I am more concerned with thought, meaning, philosophy.[57]

Since, in *State,* priority is given to what is being said the fragmented structure of the novel does not come as a surprise. Rather, the structural deformity is in keeping with the fragmented nature of the world it incorporates. *State* consists of a prologue and epilogue which enclose two short stories and a novella. Though distinct, the pieces are integrally linked to each other. The pieces examine the concept of freedom in its political, social and psychological dimensions. What differentiates *State* from the other novels discussed so far is its unique structure which is the result of the blending of literary genres like the short story, travel writing and the novella. The mingling of genres demonstrates Naipaul's conviction that forms have to be adapted to meet the demands of the author's material.[58] This innovation in the structure allows Naipaul full freedom to examine the fundamental issue of freedom with which he is concerned in the work.

In Naipaul's words *State* is a book "...about journeys, unhappy journeys by people switching countries, switching cultures."[59] In the novel the journey becomes an apt symbol for the world in flux that it portrays. The people who feature in the novel are exiles, expatriates or tourists belonging to different nationalities all of whom are far from home. In the prologue there are people belonging to nationalities as diverse as Indian, African, American, Dane, Swede, German, Chinese and Egyptian. The Egyptian Greeks are also travelling to Egypt but Egypt is no longer their home. They had been expelled from Egypt by the invaders, but finally Egypt is free and these Egyptians are the casualities of that freedom. The Tramp, in the prologue is a yet another example of the rootlessness and placelessness that is the universal crisis of the modern predicament. Till the end, the nationality of the tramp remains unfixed. For the tramp himself, nationality has ceased to have meaning. He declares: "But what's nationality these days? I myself, I think of myself as a citizen of the world."[60] For reasons that are not made clear, the tramp incurs the anger of his co-passengers with whom he shares a cabin and is beaten up. In his terror the tramp locks himself up in the cabin and threatens to set it on fire if he is not left alone. It is made clear that freedom is just an empty word in the imminent chaos that threatens to assert itself and drives people to seek safety in locked cabins. The prologue anticipates the themes to be explored in the three stories that follow and the epilogue sums up the conclusion.

The first story "one out of many" is a first person narrative in which Santosh, an Indian domestic from Bombay gives an account of his life in Washington. When the story opens he is already an American citizen, a free man and appears to have done well in life, yet he is unhappy. He yearns for his Bombay life where he had been respected and had enjoyed "a certain position."[61] Having migrated from his village he had very fast adapted himself to the city. Compared to the hard life he had led in his village as a porter, his life in Bombay as a domestic seemed to him a privileged one. He had begun to consider his life in Bombay as settled but the problem had cropped up suddenly upsetting his routined life. The problem crops up when Santosh's employer is seconded by his firm to government service and posted to Washington in the capacity of a diplomat. Santosh is faced with the threat of displacement.

Going back to his village and the porter's job is now impossible for Santosh, whom city life and its comforts have rendered unfit for hard work. However, his employer manages to get Santosh's passage sanctioned by the government and he too accompanies his employer to Washington.

In Washington, Santosh becomes aware of himself as an individual. It is his involvement with a *hubshi* (Hindi for black) woman that initiates his self-awareness which makes Santosh regard his employer and the relationship between them in a new light. He reminisces about it and acknowledges the fact that:

> Once my employer had been to me only a presence. I used to tell him then that beside him I was as dirt. It was only a way of talking, one of the courtesies of our language, but it had something of truth. I meant that he was the man who adventured in the world for me, that I experienced the world through him, that I was content to be a small part of his presence.[62]

With the self-awareness that comes to him in Washington his perspective changes altogether as he develops a critical eye:

> Now I found that, without wishing it, I was ceasing to see myself as part of my employer's presence, and beginning at the same time to see him as an outsider might see him, as perhaps the people who came to dinner in the apartment saw him. I saw that he was a man of my own age, around thirty-five; it astonished me that I hadn't noticed before. I saw that he was plump, in need of exercise, that he moved with short, fussy steps...a man who looked as uneasy in Washington as I felt, who acted as cautiously as I had learned to act.[63]

Along with the self-awareness also comes the realization that return to Bombay is now impossible for him. He can no longer be content to be a part of someone else's presence. It is as if he has just grown up and can think of his Bombay life only as "the happy times of childhood"[64] to which he no longer wished to return. His newfound psychological freedom makes him capable of independent decisions. He deserts his employer and joins Priya, an Indian who runs a restaurant there. The relationship he shares with Priya is one of comradeship and makes him feel he is back among his friends in Bombay. Working with Priya brings more than material benefits. For the first time he feels more in charge of himself than he had ever been. However, his status now, after running away from his employer, is that of an illegal immigrant and the fear of being discovered constantly nags him. He realizes that freedom brings responsibilities which he must face alone now that the security provided by the state of dependence is no longer available to him. Unable to bear the burden of his freedom, Santosh is on the verge of a breakdown and relapses into his previous psychological state of dependence. As a result his relationship with Priya undergoes a change, when instead of calling Priya by name as he had done from the beginning, he in the stupor of his fear, suddenly addresses Priya as "Sahib," thus reaffirming the master slave relationship. Santosh immediately realizes his mistake:

> I had used the wrong word. Once I had used the word a hundred times a day. But then I had considered myself a small part of my employer's presence, and the word was not servile; it was more like a name, like a reassuring sound, part of my employer's dignity and therefore part of mine. But Priya's dignity could never be mine; that was not our relationship.[65]

In the end Santosh discloses all his secrets to Priya, who then advises Santosh to marry the *hubshi* woman because that is the only way to legalize his presence in Washington. Santosh follows Priya's advice, but all that his freedom thus gained brings him is loneliness and a further fragmentation of his life into three unrelated worlds. As Santosh says: "the restaurant is one world, the parks and green streets of Washington are another, and every evening some of these streets take me to a third."[66] Ultimately all that Santosh can say about his freedom amounts to the mere fulfilment of his physical needs: "All that my freedom has brought me is the knowledge that I have a face and have a body, that I must feed this body and clothe this body for a certain number of years. Then it will be over."[67]

The next story "Tell Me Who to Kill" takes us to the West Indies, the familiar Naipaul territory. The narrator in this story is an east Indian whose plight is even more miserable than Santosh's in "One out of many." Having been denied an opportunity to make a mark in life he nurtures dreams of a better life for his brother Dayo, who becomes the obsession of his life. His self-effacement is so complete that he remains Dayo's brother till the end and is not even given a name.

In the story, Christianity is held up as the hallmark of progressiveness. The narrator tells us about his uncle, Stephen, who is educated, lives in the city and considers his Christian name as a "mark of his progressiveness." Stephen even sends his son to Montreal for furthering his studies. The narrator admires his uncle for his apparent success in life. It is only when he actually visits his uncle in the city that he discovers the dwarfish life they live:

> Now I see that in the city Stephen is not much, that all his hope and all his daughter's hope is in that son who is studying in Montreal. He is like the Prince to them. And in that little house, with no front yard and next to no backyard, they are living like Snow White and the Seven dwarfs, with their little foreign pictures in their little drawing-room, and their little pieces of polished furniture. You will feel you have to stoop, that if you take a normal step you will break something.[68]

The narrator also somehow manages to send his brother Dayo to England to study Aeronautical Engineering and later follows Dayo to London to take care of him while he is pursuing his studies. In London, the narrator feels completely lost. His life in London becomes a series of journeys to strange places:

> It is always like this now. You are always taking trains and buses to strange places. You never know what sort of street you are going to find yourself in, what sort of house you will be knocking at.[69]

Till the end the narrator remains totally unrelated to his surroundings in London. Like Stephen, who has piled all his hopes on his son all the narrator's hopes are concentrated on his brother. But when he discovers that Dayo is simply idling away his time in London, he loses all sense of direction and becomes totally lost. His mental state is well reflected in the envy he feels when he sees the tourists in London:

> But these people come for the day; they are happy, they have buses to take them back to their hotels; they have countries to go back to, they have houses. The Sadness I feel make my heart seize.[70]

The only thing that had kept him going in London was the thought that he was there for Dayo's sake, whose life he is trying to build. Dayo's failure takes the fight out of the narrator and gives him the feeling that their life in London is over. While Santosh in the preceding story is at least able to comprehend the "endless chain of action" that has led to his alienation in Washington, the narrator in this story is totally disorientated. Since coming to London he has totally lost control over his life: "I can't see where I am going. I can only wait to see what is going to turn up."[71]

Dayo represents all the people who arrive in London seeking a better future, but find that life in London is not as easy as it is believed to be. Dayo tells his brother: "It is not easy to take studies in this place as you and other people believe."[72] We cannot help feeling sympathy for Dayo, who unable to live up to the expectations of his brother becomes aimless. We learn that even Stephen's son, unable to cope with the pressure on him meets with the same fate.

Eventually, when Dayo drifts away from the narrator and marries an English girl, Dayo's brother is half-crazed with hatred but is unable to pin his enemy. He can only cry out in anguish:

> O God, show me the enemy. Once you find out who the enemy is, you can kill him. But these people here they confuse me. Who hurt me? Who spoil my life? Tell me who to beat back...tell me who to kill.[73]

Like Biswas in *House*, the narrator of this story also has a breakdown. His neurosis, like Biswas's, is the result of an intense alienation with which he just cannot cope. In fact, quite a number of Naipaul's characters suffer a breakdown.

In this connection Naipaul observes: "A person in this position [of alienation] risks going mad; I have seen it happen to others—it is a bizarre and frightening thing, and it is one of the great strands of my own writing."[74] The narrator in "Tell Me Who to Kill" is unable to locate his enemy because the enemy is not one person. "The enemy," as Naipaul points out in *Barracoon*, "is the past, of slavery and colonial neglect and a society uneducated from top to bottom. The enemy is the smallness of the islands and the absence of resources."[75]

Disillusionment with England forms the major theme of "Tell Me Who to Kill." Freedom becomes a state of being aimless and adrift, a severance of all ties with the world—a total withdrawal. The narrator who cannot bear to return home after his failure, sends back a message that he is dead. He has been reduced to a living corpse.

The title story, "In a Free State," portrays a newly independent unnamed African country in turmoil. It is set in "an English-Indian creation in the African wilderness"[76] which owes nothing to African skill. Everything in this part of Africa is supported by Americans. The major characters in the story are English. Besides some minor African characters, there is an American who makes a brief appearance. At the background of the novel is the tribal war between the tribes of the president and the king. With independence the age-old enmity between the different tribes has revived and there is a struggle for power between the president and the king. Both the king as well as the president intrigue with the local representatives of white governments for support, but the white men choose to support the president, who is in command of the new army and thus stronger than the king.

The story comes to us through the consciousness of Bobby, who is an administrative officer in one of the departments of central government and lives in the Southern Collectorate, a territory of the king's people. When the story opens, Bobby is in the capital, a four hundred mile drive from the collectorate, attending a seminar on community development. Ironically enough, there are more English participants in the seminar and the few Africans present have little to say.

On his drive back, Linda, one of the "compound wives"

joins Bobby. Though Bobby tries to remain aloof from Linda, it is not long before he is drawn into a conciliating relationship with Linda. They have conflicting views about Africa—Bobby is a liberal and demonstrates a protective attitude towards the Africans while Linda is mildly racialist. However, both share the same misconceptions about Africa. As Linda tells Bobby, before coming to the collectorate she had imagined the compound to be in "a little clearing in the forest," and had even pictured Africans "leaning on their spears under a tree and standing around one of those big old-fashioned sets. His Master's voice."[77] Bobby too confesses that he knew nothing at all about Africa and had been surprised to find them working iron.

From the scenes and incidents we witness through Bobby and Linda in the course of their long drive to the colletorate, the picture that emerges about the state of affairs in this newly independent African nation is one of total chaos. The educated Africans, who are the new men of the country, turn out to be ineffectual copies of their white benefactors. They remain as inarticulate as their brothers in the bush villages. Their lack of identity is reflected in their English-made suits and hair done in the "English style." The "bush" Africans remain in the background as a forbidding presence. When Linda and Bobby see a large number of Africans in new clothes, the former comments on their "savage" ways: "Somewhere up there they've taken off their nice new clothes and they are dancing naked and holding hands and eating dung."[78] Though this opinion comes from the racially prejudiced Linda, there is a suggestion elsewhere in the story that even the Africans who have come into contact with the white civilization will revert back to their "bush" ways. This view is put forward through the colonel who is still in charge of the tourist's resort where Bobby and Linda stop for a night. The view is substantiated by the authorial comment on the lack of co-ordination between the African soldiers and their Israeli instructor:

> But the Israeli was doing one thing, the Africans another, the Israeli was using his body, exercising, demonstrating fitness. The Africans, their eyes half closed, had fallen into a trance-like dance of the forest. Their knees hardly

> rose, their faces were blank with serious pleasure; they went blinking past the Israeli, blinking away the sweat.[79]

Even the new African officials like Sammy Kisenyi are made out to be culturally and intellectually barren. Sammy's "fatheadedness" is evidenced in his paper on broadcasting read at a conference, in which he lifts paragraphs from "T.S. Eliot, of all people."[80]

Naipaul effectively conveys the threat posed by the shifts of power which leaves no one safe. Bobby and Linda, being whites are especially vulnerable. The hunt for the king at the background, the unpredictable soldiers and the Africans, who the colonel only just manages to keep at bay, all serve to underscore the chaos that threatens to break through. The king is finally hunted down brutally and Bobby after a series of humiliations is manhandled by the president's soldiers.

The situation that prevails in Africa is conveyed through the image of the hunting dogs that have gone wild on being abandoned by their white masters. These dogs that had been used by the whites to attack Africans have now become a danger to everyone. Bobby and Linda have a narrow escape from the pack. The dogs become suggestive of the wild "free state" into which the Africans themselves have fallen after their white "masters" have left.

In the course of his long and eventful drive, Bobby has to review his attitude towards the Africans and correct his misconceptions about Africa. Bobby, no doubt is sincere when he says—"Africa saved my life"[81]—but his interest in Africa is nothing more than self-indulgence. We know that he has come to Africa after recovering from a nervous breakdown because his society has no place for homosexuals like him. In Africa Bobby sees potentials for people like him: "Africa was for Bobby the empty spaces, the safe adventure of long fatiguing drives on open roads, the other Africans, boys built like men."[82] It is difficult to miss the implication in the quoted lines. Bobby's over-friendly, patronizing attitude towards the Africans lands him into trouble a number of times. His patronizing attitude is revealed in the coaxing patios he uses with them:

> You want life? You big boy, you no go school? No, no, you no frighten. Look, I give you shilling. You hold my hand. Look, my colour, your colour. I give you shilling buy schoolbooks. Buy books, learn read, get big job. When I born again I want your colour. You no frighten. You want five shillings?[83]

A Zulu youth, who is a male-prostitute, first encourages Bobby and then spits on his face. Two other Africans, whom Bobby gives a lift in his car try to bully him. It is only Linda's anger that saves the situation. In spite of it, however, Bobby still feels protective towards them. At the filling station, the change that the African returns Bobby exceeds even the amount Bobby had given. When Linda mocks this demonstration of mindlessness, Bobby feels like hitting her. It is only when another African at the same filling station damages the windscreen of his car that he finally loses his patience and cries out angrily: "These people shouldn't be employed. They and their king have had it all their way for too long. But their little games are over now. Look at my windscreen."[84] Through this episode Naipaul tries to show that the Africans have borrowed technologies which they are unable to understand and handle. It indicates the neocolonialism at work in this newly independent African country. The interference of the whites in the internal affairs and their developmental programmes are all in reality the policies of neocolonialism. What is significant about the outburst is that Bobby demonstrates his anger only after he has recognized the offending African to be a man of the king's tribe—an already persecuted people. It is clear that Bobby knows where he stands after the scales of power have been inverted. When the president's soldiers beat him up, there is little he can do besides nursing his wounds, both physical and psychological. When Bobby gets back to the compound, Luke, his house boy laughs at him. The story concludes with Bobby realizing that he would have to leave eventually, but first he would have to dismiss Luke before whom he has been exposed. However, he can think of sacking Luke only because he belongs to the already oppressed king's Tribe.

After reading "In a Free State" one cannot help concluding that Naipaul's portrayal of Africans is banal and inauthentic.

All he has managed to do is "manufacture" after the stereotyped and dehumanized version propagated by the colonizers themselves. All the Africans portrayed in the title story are shown to be caught in certain fixed attitudes that serve only to prove certain pre-conceived notions, with no attempts made to delve into the deeper truths about this part of the colonized humanity. The few Africans who are presented to us directly are projected in an unfavourable light and only to demonstrate the points Naipaul wants to make about their "mindlessness," "mimicry" and "unpredictable nature." While the same points were also made in the case of the East Indians portrayed in the early novels, it was tinged with sympathy and understanding, which made a good deal of difference. It is surprising that Naipaul has failed to adopt the same sympathetic stance with regard to the Africans, whose colonial experience was perhaps the most brutal in the whole history of colonial violation. Throughout the story the Africans are made out to be "savage" and "barbarous." Naipaul expresses his revulsion for them by describing them as "dirty" and "smelling." Critics generally ascribe it to Naipaul's Swiftian horror of dirt. However, the context in which, Swift used such terms was entirely different and cannot be compared to the context in which Naipaul uses them.[85] Swift used them to condemn prevailing evils in the social, political and religious fields. However, he did it only in an indirect manner, by creating an imaginary land where the normal Animal vs. Human order has been inverted. Naipaul, on the other hand, dealing as he does with postcolonial subjects—an already oppressed humanity—is expected to be more sensitive and sympathetic.

In the absence of any explicitly worked out views about Africa on Naipaul's part the only option left is to glean the text and draw inferences. Apart from the views put forward through Bobby and Linda, there is a third opinion expressed by the colonel who is in charge of the tourist's resort where Bobby and Linda halt for a night. The colonel's view is an even more damaging one as it presents a completely dehumanized picture of the Africans. The colonel's attitude is clearly expressed in the following conversation between the colonel and Peter, an African youth who works for the former, in the presence of Bobby and Linda:

> 'What do you think of me, Peter?'
>
> 'I like you, Sir.'
>
> 'He likes me. Peter likes me.'
>
> 'You take me in when I was small. You give me job, you give me quarters. You look after my children.'
>
> 'He has fourteen. He's living with three of those animals right now. So polished. So nice. So well-spoken. You wouldn't believe he doesn't even know how to hold a pen in those hands. You wouldn't believe the filth he comes out of. But you like dirt, don't you Peter? You like going in to some black hole to eat filth and dance naked. You will steal and lie to do that, won't you?'
>
> 'I like the quarters, Sir.'
>
> 'While I live you will stay there. You won't move in here, Peter. I don't want you to bank on that. If I die you will starve, Peter. You will go back to bush.'
>
> 'That is true, Sir.'[86]

The passage read in conjunction with the colonel's general comment about Africa completes the dehumanization of the Africans. Speaking about Africa to Bobby and Linda, he observes: "They say there's good and bad everywhere. There's no good and bad here. They do what they have to do. That's what you have to tell yourself. You can't hate them. You can't even get angry with them. Really angry."[87] The Africans are denied even the moral sense of good and bad and it is insinuated that they are governed by the law of the jungle. It is clear that the colonel views Africa through the lens of his own culture and forms a biased opinion. One cannot help but presume that Naipaul too shares, even if partly, this broadly held eurocentric version of Africa and Africans. Otherwise he would have countered it with his own version. He does nothing of the sort. Instead, he contributes to the view, both directly through the episode in which the African soldier beat up Bobby for no logical reason and indirectly through his description of the lack of co-ordination between the African soldiers and their Israeli instructor. There seems to be no doubt after this that Naipaul is voicing his own prejudiced opinions through his characters. This is further corroborated by Naipaul's cursory dismissal of African readership in a 1979 interview where he said: "No I don't count the African readership and I don't think one should. Africa is land of bush, again not a very literary land."[88] Naipaul's prejudices quite often take on a racialist tone as is glaringly evident in the analogy he suggestively draws between the wild dogs and the Africans.

Naipaul's limitation as a postcolonial intellectual lies in the fact that he has been unable to represent the "subaltern" in the African context. As Landeg White rightly points out: "...the whole argument is conducted without any African perspective on events. Naipaul's treatment of the people who actually inhabit this country is very rudimentary."[89] Far from speaking for or making the subaltern speak, Naipaul has only muffled his voice. In Neil Lazarus's view the role of postcolonial intellectuals is "to construct a standpoint—nationalitarian, liberationist, internationalist—from which it is possible to assume the burden of speaking for all humanity."[90] Naipaul's vision falls short of such inclusiveness because he makes no attempts to understand the inner workings of the African tribal-society and its social equations, that were totally upset by colonial rule.

Naipaul focuses too much on the violence that has been unleashed after independence. As Loomba points out the "internal fractures" or "fissures"[91] that existed alongside colonialism surfaces after independence. The war between the king and the president that forms the backdrop of the title is a manifestation of internal differences. Besides, "decolonization," as frantz Fanon emphasizes, "is always a violent phenomenon."[92] It is only natural that people who were subjected to centuries of oppression and violence should themselves react with violence. Though delayed, this realization does seem to have come to Naipaul later in his career. In his article entitled "A New king for the Congo: Mobutu and the Nihilism of Africa," he defines Nihilism as "the rage of primitive people coming to themselves and finding that they have been fooled and affronted."[93]

Naipaul has been charged of an anti-Third-World bias because of his insensitive and unnecessarily brutal analysis of Third-World societies of not only the West Indies but India and Africa as well. Naipaul's reply to the charges is: "I long to find what is good and hopeful and really do hope that by the most brutal sort of analysis one is possibly opening up the situation to some sort of action; an action which is not based on self-deception."[94] "In a Free state" however, does not give the impression that Naipaul really longs to find what is good. Were it so, he would not have met with such a total negation as he does.

State concludes with an entry from Naipaul's journal entitled "The Circus at Luxor," which forms the Epilogue. In the Epilogue Naipaul makes an unexpected gesture of involvement. While in the Prologue, he had remained a detached witness to the bullying of the tramp, in the Epilogue he physically intervenes to put a stop to the drama of human misery and indignity he witnesses in Luxor. At an Oasis rest-house he sees desert children being lured by some tourists with scraps of food, which they throw on the sand. When the children draw close to get the food, a coffee-waiter scares them away with his whip. For the tourists it is an entertainment, but Naipaul is incensed by the miserable exhibition of poverty and vulnerability. He rushes to the scene and puts a stop to the act by snatching the whip from the coffee-waiter. This, indeed, is a bold gesture on Naipaul's part.

Even in Luxor, Naipaul tries to survey the landscape for a historical context by linking the present-day landscape of Egypt to the past, which exists in the form of the ruins of ancient Thebes. The first time he views the ancient ruins, he tries to get a sense of the past by isolating it from the present distress of Egypt. The landscape represented in the paintings by ancient artists speak of an ordered world whose inhabitants have a "sense of place." Naipaul concludes that such an ordered landscape could have been perceived only by "the special vision of men who knew no other land and saw what they had as rich and complete."[95] Therefore, "the muddy Nile was only water: in the paintings, a blue-green chevron: recognizable, but remote, a river in fairy land."[96] Naipaul, however, with his "stranger's eye" and knowledge of many lands finds it hard to believe that there had been such an ordered world as portrayed in the paintings on the tombs. He can only conclude: "Perhaps that vision of the land, in which the Nile was only water, a blue-green chevron, had always been a fabrication, a cause for yearning, something for the tomb."[97]

The conclusions Naipaul arrives at through his in-depth analysis of West Indian postcolonial societies are offered as the ultimate truths of all postcolonial societies. Colonial policies being more or less the same in all the colonies, no matter who the colonizers were the problems that have surfaced in the post-independence era have much in common. The economic and intellectual bankruptcy, neocolonialism and fragmentation are the major problems that all of them have to grapple with. Naipaul has been successful in conveying the effects of colonialism on the culture and psyche of the colonized. In his analysis, fragmentation, both at the macrocosmic level of the society and the microcosmic level of the individual acts as the major deterrent to progress in the post-independence period. As a result of the first, the colonized develop a split personality and lose their sense of solidity. Having lost their sense of self, they resort to mimicry in an attempt to experience a sense of wholeness and the model for mimicry is invariably an European one. Social fragmentation, on the other hand, precludes a sense of oneness which is the basic pre-requisite for the formation of a meaningful society. However, social fragmentation is the common fate of all postcolonial societies. In the case of the West Indies it is of an inherent nature, the West Indian societies being entirely the creation of empire. While in the case of countries like India, which had a traditional culture and thriving civilization prior to colonization, the social fragmentation was accelerated by colonial presence in India which thrived by reinforcing certain inherent divisions in the Indian society although on the surface it quite often presented a progressive social phase. The task of nation-building after independence becomes a major problem due to social fragmentation. Economic restructuring may be important in carrying the nation forward, but for ex-colonial societies cultural and social restructuring becomes paramount. This is the lacuna in the policies adopted by Singh's government in *Mimic*—an excessive attention was paid to economic development while the social aspect remained neglected. In such societies, where people have been reduced to economic functions, it is more important to make them aware of their social functions. Only this can provide a solid foundation from which the nation as a whole can be restructured. Naipaul shows that because of neocolonialism the economy of a country is in the hands of outside power and independence ceases to have any meaning.

In *Mimic, Flag* and *State* Naipaul has been able to delineate the idea of freedom in all its nuances. However, whether freedom is explored as a psychological category or a political reality, it is always experienced as a burden. Finally, we may conclude that in his later fiction Naipaul is obsessively preoccupied with the paradox of freedom in postcolonial societies.

REFERENCES

1. Naipaul, *Mimic*, 32.
2. Naipaul, "An Interview with V.S. Naipaul," by Adrian Rowe-Evans *Quest*, 78, Sep.-Oct. 1972: 48.
3. Naipaul, *Barracoon*, 11.
4. *Ibid.*, 16-17.
5. Naipaul, Foreword, *Finding the Centre*, by Naipaul (Harmondsworth: Penguin, 1985), 11.
6. Adrian Rowe-Evans, *Quest*, 55.
7. *Ibid.*, 55.
8. Naipaul, "The Documentary Heresy," *Critical Perspectives on V.S. Naipaul*, 24.
9. Andrew Gurr, *Writers in Exile: the Creative Use of Home in Modern Literature* (Sussex: The Harvester Press, 1981), 86.
10. Andrew Gurr, *Writers in Exile*, 86.
11. Naipaul, "The Novelist Talks About his world," by Ronald Bryden, *Listener*, 22 Mar. 1973: 367.
12. Naipaul, *Area*, 42.
13. Naipaul, *Mimic*, 251.
14. Naipaul, interview, "The Novelist V.S. Naipaul. Talks to Nigel Bingham about His Childhood in Trinidad," *Listener*, 7 Sep. 1972: 307.
15. Naipaul, *Mimic*, 5.
16. John Cooke, "A vision of the Land: V.S. Naipaul's later novels," *Caribbean Quarterly* 25.4 (1979): 32.

17. Naipaul, *Mimic*, 171-72.
18. *Ibid.*, 50.
19. Naipaul, *State*, 179-80.
20. William Walsh, *V.S. Naipaul* (Edinburgh: Oliver and Boyd, 1973), 62.
21. Naipaul, *Mimic*, 83.
22. *Ibid.*, 97.
23. *Ibid.*, 95.
24. *Ibid.*, 111.
25. *Ibid.*, 151.
26. *Ibid.*, 118.
27. *Ibid.*, 125.
28. *Ibid.*, 129.
29. *Ibid.*, 132.
30. *Ibid.*, 140.
31. *Ibid.*, 153.
32. *Ibid.*, 27.
33. *Ibid.*, 100.
34. *Ibid.*, 55
35. *Ibid.*, 57.
36. *Ibid.*, 80.
37. *Ibid.*, 8.
38. *Ibid.*, 204.
39. *Ibid.*, 192.
40. *Ibid.*, 216.
41. *Ibid.*, 215.
42. *Ibid.*, 206.
43. *Ibid.*, 210.
44. Madhusudana Rao, *Contrary Awareness*, 43.
45. Naipaul, *Flag*, 132.
46. *Ibid.*, 154.
47. *Ibid.*, 175.
48. *Ibid.*, 168.
49. *Ibid.*, 181.
50. *Ibid.*, 182.
51. *Ibid.*, 206.
52. *Ibid.*, 199.
53. *Ibid.*, 165.
54. *Ibid.*, 165.
55. *Ibid.*, 164.

56. Naipaul, *State*, 10.
57. Naipaul, "Delivering the Truth," *Times Literary Supplement* 2 Sep. 1994: 3-4.
58. Adrean Rowe-Evans, "An Interview with V.S. Naipaul," *Quest* Sep.-Oct. 1972: 54.
59. Jim Douglas Henry, "Unfurnished Entrails," *Listener* 25 Nov. 1971: 721.
60. Naipaul, *State*, 11.
61. *Ibid.*, 25.
62. *Ibid.*, 40.
63. *Ibid.*, 41.
64. *Ibid.*, 45.
65. *Ibid.*, 52.
66. *Ibid.*, 60-61.
67. *Ibid.*, 61.
68. *Ibid.*, 81.
69. *Ibid.*, 86.
70. *Ibid.*, 99.
71. *Ibid.*, 66.
72. *Ibid.*, 96.
73. *Ibid.*, 107.
74. Adrian Rowe Evans, *Quest*, 52.
75. Naipaul, *Baracoon*, 271.
76. Naipaul, *State*, 111.
77. *Ibid.*, 122-23.
78. *Ibid.*, 173.
79. *Ibid.*, 180-81.
80. *Ibid.*, 225.
81. *Ibid.*, 124.
82. *Ibid.*, 117.
83. *Ibid.*, 117.
84. *Ibid.*, 156.
85. Jonatham Swift, *Gulliver's Travels*, (London: Penguin, 1994), 253-63.
86. Naipaul, *State*, 189.
87. *Ibid.*, 193.
88. Naipaul, "A conversation with V.S. Naipaul," by Robert Boyers and Bharati Mukherjee *Salmagundi*, 54 (1981): 6.
89. Landeg White, V.S. Naipaul: A Critical Introduction, 200.
90. Neil Lazarus, "National Consciousness And Intellectualism," eds. Francis

Barker, Hulme and Iversem, *Colonial Discourses/Postcolonial Theory* (Manchester: Manchester University Press, 1994), 220.

91. Ania Loomba, *Colonialism/Postcolonialism*, (London: Routledge, 1998), 11.
92. Frantz Fanon, *The Wretched of the Earth*, trans. Constance Farrington (Harmondsworth: Penguin, 1967), 27.
93. Naipaul, *Return*, 187.
94. Adrian Rowe-Evans, *Quest*, 51.
95. Naipaul, *State*, 251.
96. *Ibid.*, 251.
97. *Ibid.*, 256.

5

NAIPAUL'S VISION OF THE WORLD IN *GUERRILLAS* AND *A BEND IN THE RIVER*

I feel that to destroy the world is the only course of action that is now open to sane men.[1]

—V.S. Naipaul

Nobody's going anywhere. We're all going to hell, and every man knows this in his bones.[2]

—V.S. Naipaul

A striking feature that characterizes Naipaul's later fiction beginning with *Mimic* upto *Bend* is its intensely political nature. While it is true that, of his earlier novels, *Masseur* dealt with a politician of sorts and *Elvira* was constructed around a major political event, the novels served mainly to highlight the social tensions inherent in the colonial world which they portrayed. It would be fair to say that Naipaul at this stage of his career was not a political writer in any conscious sense. The same however, cannot be said about his later novels where there is a clear shift of focus to the post-imperial Third World political scenario, so much so that individuals are reduced to political beings and the social situation as a whole is described in terms of power politics. Every relationship, even the one between the sexes is affected by it. This aspect first manifests itself in *Mimic*. The novel has already been discussed in the preceding chapter and we may recall that Singh experiences either a sense of triumph or defeat in his various encounters with women. Later on, his marriage also breaks down because the racial difference between him and his English wife suddenly asserts itself. In his last two novels that are taken up for discussion in this chapter, *Guerrillas* and *Bend*, politics dominates sexual relations to such an extent that it ends up in misogynist violence. In the first sexual encounter between Jane, the English liberal and Jimmy, the half-caste, self-styled Black Power leader in *Guerrillas*, the former insults the latter by asserting her racial superiority over him. In their second encounter Jimmy sodomizes Jane and then offers her to Bryant, who murders her. Salim in *Bend* experiences an anxiety as he realizes that the future of his relationship with Yvette, Raymond's wife, depends on the president who governs everybody's lives. This relationship too ends in bitterness. In fact, as Hana Wirth-Nesher observes: "Sexuality in Naipaul's fiction is contrary to that literary tradition in which nakedness implies stripping men and women of their cultural and political roles as well."[3] Indeed, in the post-imperial world political identities become so integral a part of life that intimacy becomes an impossibility. Every sexual relationship forged in the novel is of a perverse nature.

It was mentioned in the previous chapter that Naipaul's novels become progressively bleak. This tendency reaches its climax in *Guerrillas* and *Bend*. These novels hold up an utterly desolate vision of the world. In *Guerrillas*, desolation is writ large on the landscape itself. Set in a drought-ridden Caribbean island *Guerrillas* opens into what sounds like Eliot's "Waste Land:"

> The sea smelled of swamp; it barely rippled, had glitter rather than colour; and the heat seemed trapped below the pink haze of bauxite dust from the bauxite loading station. After the market, where refrigerated trailers were unloading; after the rubbish dump burning in the remnant of mangrove swamp, with black carrion corbeaux squatting hunched on fence-posts or hopping about on the ground; after the built-up hillsides; after the new housing estates, rows of unpainted boxes of concrete and corrugated iron already returning to the shanty towns that had been knocked down for this redevelopment; after the naked children playing in the red dust of the straight new avenues, the clothes hanging the rags from backyard lines; after this, the land cleared a little. And it was possible to see over what the city had spread: on one

> side, the swamp, drying out to a great plain; on the other side, a chain of hills, rising directly from the plain.[4]

The people who inhabit this "waste land" are quite in tune with it. They are derelicts, morally and intellectually barren. The physical deformity of the landscape finds its human parallel in Bryant, a physically as well as mentally deformed youth, who is one of Jimmy's boys in the agricultural commune. In contrast to the arid barrenness of the landscape presented in *Guerrillas*, the landscape of *Bend* has a choking fertility but the vision of the world remains essentially the same. It is the vision of a world undoing itself. Naipaul's last novel, *Bend* too holds out little hope for the world and ends on the terrifying thought that "nowhere is safe now."[5]

The major Naipaulian themes of identity crisis, displacement, homelessness, marginality and neocolonialism reach their culmination in these two novels even as Naipaul exposes the Black Power movement of the imaginary Caribbean island in *Guerrillas* and probes into the dynamics of race politics in *Bend*.

One point that needs to be made about *Bend* is the noticeable change in Naipaul's treatment of African characters. In the preceding chapter while discussing *State* we had discussed the limitations in Naipaul's presentation of Africa and African characters, which could not have been the outcome of a detailed enquiry and analysis. In *Bend* however, there is a considerable difference in his treatment of Africa. Not only is he more sympathetic but there is a sincere attempt on his part to analyse and arrive at an understanding of the problems that grip post-independence Africa. His portrayal of African characters caught in the slipstream of history has also been done in a convincing manner.

Guerrillas is set in an unnamed Caribbean island and the action centres around three major characters—Jimmy, Jane and Roche. The novel is based on the real life character of Michael X also known as Abdul Malik, whose story Naipaul had published in *Return*, his collection of articles. In the fictional account however, Naipaul makes some changes in the cast in order to extend its thematic possibilities by introducing two new characters—Roche the white liberal and

Bryant, a black homosexual youth—and transforms the original story into a modern fable of power and marginality. Roche's presence in the island as Jimmy's "master" emphasizes the persistence of colonialism in the era of political independence in the Caribbean islands. In fact, real power still resides outside the Island and everyone living in it including Roche and Jane are at the margins of power. Bryant, apart from being Jimmy's alterego—the person Jimmy feels he has not yet escaped being—adds a fresh dimension to the theme of marginality. Being a slum youth, who is physically deformed and barely articulate, one would think of him as the most marginal character in the novel. Yet, he can bully Jane and extort a dollar from her. Later on, he even becomes a party to her murder. The incidents highlight the fact that in a male dominated world Jane's position as a woman is even more marginal than Bryant's.

The title of the novel suggests a lot of action but the political situation is rendered not directly through political action but obliquely through the psychological reflexes of individuals drawn into the vortex of revolution.[6] Naipaul employs the Third person omniscient narrator's perspective and successfully dramatizes the degenerate politics of the post-independence ex-colony as he moves in and out of the consciousness of his characters. The story-line of the novel runs thus: Jimmy Ahmed, just returned from London after involving himself in sexual assault is feared by everyone. The government fears him because of his "English glamour" while capitalistic firms like the "Sablich's" who have investments in the island fear him as a Black Power man who can bring about a revolution in the land. Jimmy knows his potentials only too well: "They've got to support me.... Because, if I fail-hmm. I'm the only man that stands between them and revolution and they know it now, massa. That's why I'm the only man they're afraid of."[7] The affluent capitalists realize that in order to keep Jimmy from creating trouble for them, they must harness his latent energy and channelize it. The agricultural commune is meant to encourage and employ the idle energies of the island. Jimmy calls the commune "Thrushcross Grange" and leads the slum youths to bring about a revolution based on land. Peter Roche is the man hired by the Sablich's as their social worker to supervise over the project. Roche has a background that recommends him as the best man for the job: He is a white liberal, who has been tortured in South Africa for his involvement in the anti-apartheid cause. Thus, he is the ideal public relations man for the Sablich's especially because of their unsavoury past as a slave trading firm. Jane is Roche's girlfriend, who has followed him to the island because she believes Roche to be an "engaged doer." However, it does not take long for her to realize that Roche's position in the island is no better than that of a refugee. Her disillusionment with Roche takes her to Jimmy but the relationship takes off on a wrong footing with Jane dominating over Jimmy on their first sexual encounter and incurring his hatred.

In the meanwhile the situation in the island becomes explosive when Stephen, one of the inmates of the commune, who had been missing for some time is killed by the police. Jimmy carries the body around the town and picks up a big procession. Violence breaks out as the mob becomes riotous. Chaos prevails and the police unable to control the mob withdraws. However, normalcy returns when the American planes arrive to take control of the situation. Jimmy gets a rude shock when the mob reject his leadership and he realizes that he is a finished man. Jane and Roche too decide to leave the island. Jane goes to meet Jimmy before going away and Jimmy, frustrated as he is, subjects Jane to an indecent insult and offers her to Bryant, who kills her. Roche helps Jimmy to erase all evidence about Jane's presence in the island and escapes to London leaving Jimmy alone.

The dual role of the narrator as an "involved witness and omniscient observer"[8] provides Naipaul ample scope and full freedom to delineate his characters in a vivid and subtle manner. Most of the characters are made available to us directly as the narrator enters their consciousness and exposes them. There is an ironic contrast between what the characters think and feel, and what they say and do. In addition to the peep we get into the psyche of the characters, they are subjected to further assessment through their perceptions about one another. For instance, Jane initially thinks of Roche as a "doer" and the island as the setting for his action. However, the image of Roche that Jane nurtures in her mind is shattered when on coming to the island she perceives that:

> ...on the island, which in her imagination had once been the setting of action that would undo the world, Roche was a refugee. He was a man who didn't have a place to go back to; he was someone for whom room had been made.[9]

Likewise, Roche's idea about Jane also undergoes a change after she joins him at the Ridge. When he had first met her in London he had considered her to be a coherent person with a point of view. Later it becomes clear to him that:

> All that was to be known about her was clear at that first meeting: it was her total display. But what London had masked the Ridge now, too late, made plain. How often in London, he had seen her casual irritations and hostility mistaken, as they had been mistaken by him, for a point of view. How easy it had been in that city for her simple impressionistic comments, borrowed from here and there, and some already borrowed from himself and distorted to suggest a complete and coherent personality.[10]

Thus both Jane and Roche are revealed to be decentred human beings who having ventured into the Third World in search of a cause have become disoriented. However, the narrators's approach towards his male characters is essentially sympathetic and they are presented as victims of their circumstances. This is true in the case of the physically repulsive Bryant, as well as the murderous Jimmy and both emerge as equally pathetic figures. Bryant, in spite of his threatening appearance is sensitive enough to cry when while watching his favourite Poitier film he realizes the potentials that have gone wasted in him:

> Watching the film, he began to grieve for what was denied him: that future in which he became what he truly was, not a man with a gun, a big profession or big talk but himself, and as himself was loved and readmitted to the house and to the people in the house. He began to sob....[11]

Jimmy too, for all the aura of power that surround him, turns out to be a mere play thing in the hands of the radical groups that patronize him. This reality becomes apparent in Jimmy's correspondence with a man called Roy which lays bare his inner feeling of insecurity and vulnerability. Incidentally, the letter is written before the riots actually break out:

> The situation is desperate Roy, the people here have been betrayed too often, it's always a case of black faces white masks, you don't know who your enemy is, the enemy infiltrates your ranks all the time. Massa Mister Roche he's very importunate in his inquiries about one of the boys they sent here, Stephen a little gang leader from the city, a big coup for them, they thought he was going to take over from me.... But the situation is getting desperate now, in the still of the night I lose my courage, I feel it's a losing battle, they're sending other agents, I don't know how to cope.[12]

However, in the case of Jane's character we find a total lack of sympathy on Naipaul's part. Even the description of the murder scene is done in a passionless, clinical manner.

Jimmy's character is meant as a foil to expose the farce and futility of the Black Power movements in the Caribbean islands. When the riots break out, Jimmy as a rejected leader is no longer in a position to control it. In fact in the utter confusion that breaks loose, even the police "don't know who they fighting or who they fighting for."[13] Everyone seems to be a leader. Ultimately, it is the Americans who impose order to protect their own mercenary interest in the island's bauxite.

The title of the novel carries ironic overtones which are made clear in the ineffectual way the guerrillas presented in the novel function. Naipaul shows that in inorganic and racially divided societies like the Caribbean there can be no authentic internal source of power. This is an oft-repeated idea in Naipaul's novels. In a picaroon society like the one depicted in the novel, everyone is a guerrilla—a "privateer—"[14] fighting for his own little cause. The guerrillas we meet—Roche, Jane, Jimmy and the boys at the commune—are derelicts who have no sense of purpose in life and only just "carry-on." Contrary to being people who shape events, they are people who placidly wait for events to give shape to their amorphous lives. Roche lacks conviction in the revolution based on land that his firm seeks to promote and even thinks of it as "anti-historical."[15] Yet, he accepts the job only because it provides him with an opportunity to escape from London, where his life is under threat. For a guerrilla, he makes a very controversial statement when Jane asks him whether he feels no bitterness about the torture he was subjected to in jail. His deflating answer is: "You must understand I have always accepted authority."[16]

Jimmy, who professes to be the leader of the black power movement in the island is no more genuine than the others. His half-caste status renders his position as the leader extremely ironical. As Meredith, the political drop-out tells Roche while interviewing him being half-Chinese Jimmy could not have been in tune with the aspirations of black people. The mark of a genuine guerrilla movement is the clear distinction it makes between the rightful, native culture and the illegitimate power of the occupying "other."[17] But Jimmy is incapable of drawing the line between the two because he is a cultural schizophrenic. This is first evident in the interior decoration of his home which mimicks English middle-class suburbia to such an extent that Jane, on her first visit, cries out: "But its like being in England."[18] So complete is his grounding in English society that he even adopts the mask of an English woman in the novel he is writing. Again, the name of his commune, "Thrushcross Grange" is borrowed from Emily Bronte's novel Wuthering Heights. Jimmy is the archetypal, Naipaulian mimic man. If the leadership is such the following can be nc better than it is: Bryant and all the boys at the commune are human debris "spawned by the city, casually conceived, and after the backyard drama and ritual of their birth gradually abandoned...."[19] Jane is presented as the least authentic character: "She was only what she did or said at any given moment."[20] She is full of "unrelated ideas deposited in her soul as she had adventured in life, the debris of a dozen systems she had picked up from a dozen men."[21] When she becomes involved with Jimmy her intuition warns her that she is playing with fire, yet she persists in her involvement with Jimmy because she thinks she is privileged enough to leave the island whenever she wishes. This turns out to be another of her many misconceptions and she meets her gruesome end.

Naipaul's apocalyptic vision offers an extremely dismal view of the world. It envisions the post-imperial world as falling apart. At the end of *Mimic*, it was still possible for the narrator to "clear the decks" and make a fresh beginning. But in *Guerrillas* and *Bend* Naipaul is at the nadir of his hopes. Naipaul makes it explicit that "no one will make a fresh start or do anything new."[22] The world contained in *Guerrillas* is on the brink of extinction and this is evident in the Ridge, the city and the commune, all of which are described in terms of decay. The houses on the Ridge are not homes but "concrete shells." As Jane notes, these houses would never become "like family houses that had been lived in for two or three generations."[23] Harry Tunga appears to be a happily settled, Ridge man but even his apparently cosy little world is breaking up. His wife's leaving him for another man signifies the spiritual barrenness that has set in. The fact that Harry has been quietly securing his escape from the island by acquiring a landed immigrant status for himself in Canada comes as a startling news for Jane and Roche.

Down in the city, the community has already collapsed and what remains is "a community without rules."[24] This disorder of the city threatens to "spread up and up, through roads and woodland, and eventually overwhelm"[25] the seemingly secure Ridge. The impermanence of the world is reinforced through Jimmy's realization that: "there are no more mansions. I suppose like everyone else I fooled myself that there was a mansion waiting somewhere for me...."[26] To Naipaul the Post-imperial world has no centre. Both the former colonizers as well as the colonized are at the margins of power but each identifies the center with the other.

Like the quests for identity and freedom, Naipaul's characters' search for power also meets with failure. For Jimmy the quest ends in a fiasco and for Jane it proves to be fatal. Roche only just manages to escape from the island and save himself. Finally, it is Meredith, the colonial politician who becomes the minister. However, the events that lead to his becoming the minister are so vaguely presented that one cannot derive any positive meaning out of it. It only reiterates the unpredictable and chaotic nature of politics in the Third World.

On the whole, the mood that haunts the novel is one of existential despair. As Sashi Kamra observes: "It is similar to existential absurdity: of anguish at living in an unrelated meaningless world: in a void."[27] Pessimism, a central strain in Naipaul's oeuvre, takes on a relentless intensity in the last two novels. This reflects a major personal crisis in Naipaul's life—his disillusionment with India. His visits to India convinced him that his long cherished dream of a home in his ancestral land had been a folly. In the foreword to *India: A Wounded Civilization,* Naipaul records the disappointment thus: "In India I know I am a stranger; but increasingly I understand that my Indian memories of that India which lived on in my childhood in Trinidad, are like trapdoors into a bottomless past."[28] This explains the pervasive idea of exile and lostness as a universal condition in his novels.

Upto *House* Naipaul's major concern was to reconstruct his past and establish his home identity because a home was then perceived as a precondition for identity; homelessness was thus viewed as a major limitation. Subsequent to his failure with India however, Naipaul began to perceive the concepts of identity and home in a new light. Homelessness was now seen as a boon rather than a bane because a whole world of possibilities opens up to people without a side. This idea is put across most forcefully in *Bend.* Like *Guerrillas, Bend* is yet another example of travel writing transmuted into fiction. The novel has emerged from his long article entitled "A New King for the Congo: Mobutu and the Nihilism of Africa"[29] published in *Return,* in which Naipaul analyses post-colonial Zaire. By setting the novel in the wider context of Africa, Naipaul broadens the perspective of the themes he has here-to-fore developed. It is Naipaul's notable achievement that "he has made the Caribbean experience an integral strand in the pattern of human condition."[30]

Bend is set in an unnamed African country undergoing political ferment. However the landscape with the river, the rapids, the steamer service and the close modelling of the Big man's character on Mobutu as well as the events described make it obvious that the unnamed country is no other than Congo or Zaire. In *Bend,* Naipaul's major themes converge to reveal the disturbing realities of post-imperial Zaire. Throughout Naipaul's work there is an emphasis on the importance of history both private and public. The identity crisis that his characters face is due to the obliteration of their past and those who eventually overcome the crisis are the ones who have recovered their past or somehow managed to "impose an order" on their own histories. In *Bend,* although a sense of the past is still important, at the same time it is clear that there can be no return to the past. To the exile the past can only cause pain, so it is necessary to learn to "trample on the past...."[31]

The world Naipaul meditates upon in *Bend* is Conrad's "heart of darkness" but with a difference in perspective. Conrad in *Heart of Darkness* had dealt with the deterioration of the white man's morale from idealism to savagery consequent to his coming into contact with "wilderness, solitude and power."[32] Naipaul does quite the opposite. He depicts what the insubstantial kind of civilization brought by Europe does to the Africans:

> But the man with the inconceivable mystery of a soul that knew no restraint, no faith, and no fear was black and not white; and he had been maddened not by contact with wilderness and primitivism, but with the civilization established by those pioneers who now lie on Mont Ngaliema, above the kinshasa rapids.[33]

In *Bend* Naipaul focuses on the "African contradictions" which are the outcome of the contact with Western civilization. The Bigman in *Bend* embodies this contradiction in his revival of the African worship of ancestors through the "cult of the mother" even as he fashions his modern Africa at the Domain. The Domain with its shoddy grandeur has not come out of Africa and is as alien as the water hyacinth that has "floated up from the south, seeding itself as it travelled."[34]

In Naipaul's Africa the situation is further complicated by a new destructive force: African Nihilism, which Naipaul describes as "the rage of primitive men coming to themselves and finding that they have been fooled and affronted."[35] The second rebellion that the first section of the novel describes, as well as the liberation army that proclaims itself in the later part of the novel exhibit the nihilistic impulses that seek to destroy everything that is not of the forest and Africa. During the second rebellion the town at the bend in the river is destroyed because it is a reminder of "the intruders who had ruled in it and from it...."[36] The Liberation Army seeks to overthrow the Bigman's regime and revive the old ways. To achieve this they seek to exterminate "every body who can read and write everybody who ever put on a jacket and tie... all the masters and all the servants."[37] In the violence that breaks out the expatriates and immigrants find themselves in an extremely vulnerable position. *Bend* centres around Salim, an East Indian muslim, whose family though settled in Africa for generations are still considered as outsiders. Salim belongs to a community that is basically ahistorical:

> We never asked why; we never recorded. We felt in our bones that we were a very old people; but we seemed to have no means of guaging the passing of time. Neither my father nor grandfather could put dates to their stories. Not because they had forgotten or were confused; the past was simply the past.[38]

Whatever little Salim knows of his past is from books written by Europeans. Salim realizes that without Europeans all their past "would have been washed away...."[39] Salim, having developed the habit of conscious self-assessment because of his Western education realizes that his community has fallen behind. He awakens to the anomaly of their position in the coast. Even Indar, his East Indian, Hindu friend arrives at the same insight. He tells Salim: "We are washed up here, you know. To be in Africa you have to be strong. We are not strong. We don't even have a flag."[40] Salim is prompted into action when Indar tells him that he is leaving for England. He decides to break away from his family and make a new beginning elsewhere and when Nazruddin, a man belonging to his community, offers him a shop and business in the town at the bend he readily accepts.

When Salim arrives at the town he finds it destroyed by the tribal war that has just swept by. Salim is unnerved to see the ruins which speak of "the depth of that African rage, the wish to destroy, regardless of the consequences."[41] It unsettles him to see the ruined suburb near the rapids, valuable real estate only recently being reclaimed by the bush. In the midst of ruins that look like relics of a dead civilization, Salim feels like "a ghost, not from the past, but from the future."[42] Salim finds himself trapped once again in the same situation from which he had sought his escape from the coast. It is clear that there can be no fresh beginnings anywhere. Neither is it now possible for Salim to return to the coast because in the meanwhile due to an uprising in the coast Salim's family too has had to scatter and Metty, a family slave is sent to stay with him.

At the town, Salim comes to know three Indian families and becomes especially close with Mahesh and Shoba. The only Africans he comes into direct contact with are Zabeth, his customer and her son Ferdinand, whose guardianship Zabeth entrusts to Salim. Ferdinand attends the lycee but Salim sees that the education he receives at the lycee only confuses Ferdinand and fills his mind with "all kinds of junk."[43] This serves as a scathing comment on the quality of education given in missionary schools like the lycee.

Father Huismans, the lycee's Belgian headmaster, has deep interest in African cultural artifacts. He makes expeditions into the interior villages to collect African masks and carvings. Indifferent to the political situation, he sees the destruction of the town as only a temporary set back—as things that happened "when something big and new was being set up, when the course of history was being altered."[44] In spite of his reputation as a lover of Africa, he has a reverence for "everything connected with European colonization."[45] He sees true Africa as "dying or about to die"[46] and as its last lucky witness seeks to collect and preserve its cultural artifacts. It is Father Huismans who interprets to Salim the meaning of the two Latin mottos that had puzzled Salim. The first is also the motto of the lycee and reads: *Semper aliquid novi*. These are the words of an ancient Roman writer who had written that out of Africa there was "always something new."[47] The second motto is the one Salim had seen inscribed on the ruined monument near the dock gates: *Miscerique probat populos et foedera jungi.* The words mean that the Roman god "approves of the mingling of the people and their bonds of union."[48] The lines are a corruption of the original lines that occur in virgil's Aeneid in the Aeneas-Dido episode. Dido, the African queen falls in love with the Roman hero and there is a contemplation about the possibility of their union. Then the watching gods take a hand and one of them says that the great "Roman god might not approve of a settlement in Africa, of a mingling of peoples there, of treaties of union between Africans and Romans."[49] This reflects the vain-gloriousness of the colonizers, who had twisted the two thousand year old lines to celebrate sixty years of steamer service. As the ruins testify, there can be no mingling of the people and any attempts to do so would only end in destruction. Father Huismans's brutal killing is a further proof of the fact. This happens just after the army quells another tribal uprising. During the early days of peace, Father Huismans goes on one of his trips to the interior and meets his gruesome death: "His body had been mutilated, his head cut off and spiked."[50]

To Salim and the others, Father Huismans's death comes as a warning that they have to be careful and remember that they are in Africa. The mechanical and superficial nature of the social life in the town which continues unruffled even after Father Huismans's death is very well evoked in the image of the column of ants:

> If you look at a column of ants on the march you will see that there are some who are stragglers or have lost their way. The column has no time for them; it goes on. Sometimes the stragglers die. But even this has no effect on the column. There is a little disturbance around the corpse, which is eventually carried off and then it appears so light. And all the time the great business continues, and that apparent sociability, that rite of meeting and greeting which ants travelling in opposite directions, to and from their nest, perform without fail.
>
> So it was after the death of Father Huismans.[51]

However, Father Huismans's prediction that "there would always be a settlement at that bend in the river"[52] proves to be true. The town is not only re-established but begins to grow under the regime of the Big Man:

> All kinds of projects were started. Various government departments came to life again, and the town at last became a place that could be made to work. We already had the steamer service; now the airfield was re-commissioned and extended, to take the jets from the capital (and to fly in soldiers).... We even began to get a new telephone system. It was far too elaborate for our needs, but it was what the Big man in the capital wanted for us.[53]

The most stupendous project, however is the "State Domain." Being built on the ruins it is the Big Man's miracle carrying the message that "Africans had become modern men who built in concrete and glass and sat in cushioned chairs covered in imitation velvet."[54] That modernization is only another form of mimicry is made obvious in the quoted lines. It is ironical that no one knows what the Domain is being built for and it is only after its completion that a use is found for it: It is made a "university city and a research centre." Ferdinand joins it on a government scholarship after finishing at the lycee.

Salim's own feelings about the Domain are mixed and complicated. While he knows that the shoddy grandeur is a hoax, he cannot help envying Ferdinand for having admittance into the world of the Domain:

> Yet I couldn't help thinking how lucky Ferdinand was, how easy it had been made for him. You took a boy out of the bush and you taught him to read and write; you levelled the bush and built a polytechnic and you sent him there. It seemed easy as that; if you came late to the world and found ready made those things that other countries and peoples had taken so long to arrive at—writing, printing, universities, books, knowledge. The rest of us had to take things in stages.... Ferdinand, starting from nothing, had with one step made himself free, and was ready to race ahead of us.[55]

After Ferdinand has left for the polytechnic, Salim discovers that Metty has a family somewhere in town. He feels betrayed and his own loneliness makes him reflect on the desolation of the world where it is no longer possible to have a settled life:

> ...Nothing stands still. Everything changes. I will inherit no house, and no house that I build will now pass to my children. That way of life has gone. I have lost my twenties, and what I have been looking for since I left home hasn't come to me. I have only been waiting. I will wait for the rest of my life.[56]

At this point Indar re-enters Salim's life. He comes to the town as the government's guest at the Domain. It is through Indar that Salim meets Raymond, the president's "white man" and his wife Yvette. Salim is dazzled by the glamorous life of the Domain. Soon after, an affair develops between Salim and Yvette revitalizing Salim. In the course of his affair with Yvette Salim discovers the reality behind the glamorous life Raymond and Yvette seem to live. Yvette reveals her fears and frustration regarding their uncertain future because of the indifferent attitude the Big Man has adopted towards them. When Yvette tells Salim that her life is still fluid while his is settled, he realizes that no one has certainties of any kind.

Meanwhile Nazruddin's letter brings more disturbing news. Racial troubles having broken out in Uganda as well, Nazruddin has had to shift his family yet again. Nazruddin's plan to move out of Africa and go to Canada makes it clear that no African country is free of troubles. Nazruddin's letter shows how modernization has been responsible for the outbreak of violence in Africa:

> The motorcar and modern roads had made the country too small; there would always be trouble. Every tribe felt more threatened in its territory now than in the days when everybody, including traders from the coast like our grandfathers, went about on foot, and a single trading venture could take up to a year. Africa, going back to its old ways with modern tools, was going to be a difficult place for sometime.[57]

Meanwhile, the situation in the town worsens as a liberation Army announces itself. This time there is a lot of violence and bloodshed in the town itself. The external chaos puts a strain on Salim and Yvette's relationship, which finally ends up in a disgusting manner with Salim insulting Yvette. Salim leaves for England and gets engaged to Nazruddin's daughter. He decides to wind-up his business in the town and make a fresh beginning. On returning to the town however, he comes to know that his shop has been taken over by the state under the new policy of "radicalization." Citizen Theotime is the state trustee in charge of the shop and Salim has to become Theotime's manager. In his desperate attempt to get out of the place Salim gets involved in the illegal Ivory trade, is caught and put into prison. He is saved by Ferdinand, who turns out to be the new commissioner and arranges for his escape. Ferdinand's parting words to Salim encapsulate Naipaul's vision of the world:

> You mustn't think it's bad just for you. It's bad for everybody. That's the terrible thing. It's bad for Prosper, bad for the man they gave your shop to, bad for everybody. Nobody's going anywhere. We're all going to hell, and every man knows this in his bones. We're being killed. Nothing has any meaning. That is why everyone is frantic. Everyone wants to make his money and run away. But where? That is what is driving people mad. They feel they're losing the place they can run back to...nowhere is safe now.[58]

In spite of the pessimistic vision that *Bend* imposes, it's human concern makes it a much more rewarding novel compared to *Guerrillas*. Through the rich array of characters, Naipaul is successful in delineating the complexities of modern life. Naipaul demonstrates his dexterity in his sensitive handling of Ferdinand's character. Ferdinand represents the modern African who has been picked from bush life only to be placed in a more vulnerable position in the civilized jungle of the town, which provides no sanctuary or protection. The Big Man, though not physically present looms large in the big photographs put up everywhere. He is a typical example of the "Black Man" who has assumed the "lies of white men."[59] Through Indar and Salim, Naipaul portrays the plight of the displaced exiles who have nowhere to go. Raymond and Yvette demonstrate that in the new dynamics of power, everyone is in a marginal position. Through Raymond, Naipaul also exposes the lack of authenticity in the articles on historical events like the ones Raymond is writing. When Salim goes through Raymond's article about the race riot, he notes that after the bright opening the article had turned out to be "a compilation of government decrees and quotations from newspapers."[60] Raymond himself acknowledges the difficulty of writing about "what has never been written before."[61] He considers Theodore Mommsen as the giant of modern historical writing, and everything written about the Roman Republic is only a continuation of Mommsen. The reason Raymond provides corroborates, once again, Naipaul's vision of the world:

> Theodore Mommsen had the comfort of knowing that his subject was a great one. Those of us who work in our particular field have no such assurance. We have no idea of the value posterity will place on the events we attempt to chronicle. We have no idea where the continent is going. We can only carry on.[62]

Naipaul's vision offers little hope to Third World societies that have been maimed beyond repair. However, through his depiction of London in *Bend*, he puts forward the view that displacement and alienation are a universal predicament in the post-war world and one must learn to live with this ultimate truth. Salim arrives at this piece of wisdom the hard way and he decides to rejoin the world because: "The World is what it is; men who are nothing, who allow themselves to be nothing, have no place in it."[63] It is clear that Naipaul holds the postcolonial subjects totally responsible for their condition. Naipaul can see little good coming out of native liberation movements. Due to internal fractures in postcolonial societies, native liberation movements fail to play a positive role in the formation of an authentic Third World consciousness. In none of his works therefore, does Naipaul offer collective action as a possible solution to the colonial condition. In Naipaul's terms then, the solution is to be had at the individual level through self-decolonization, that is by overcoming the colonial mentality of idleness and irresponsibility. In *Bend*, though Naipaul seems sympathetic to the African impulse to destroy all the physical reminders of the European presence, he, at the same time makes it clear that destruction of surface features alone is not sufficient. As Anthony Boxill puts it: "Violence to what is mimic and inferior within the personality, is what is necessary."[64] The difference between Jimmy and Salim lies in the fact that the former is unable to break away from the colonial state of dependence and vents out his frustration on Jane in an empty gesture of violence whereas, Salim, because of his acquired habit of self-appraisal knows where exactly he stands, and this insight makes him take the positive step of rejoining the world. *Bend* concludes with Naipaul's failure to arrive at any positive conclusion about Africa, which according to him is a "land of bush."[65]

Having come to the end of the discussion of Naipaul's works, it is important, at this point, to examine an aspect of Naipaul's work that has so far remained unexplored: Naipaul's treatment of women in his fiction. It has been pointed out by critics that Naipaul treats the women characters in his later fiction rather harshly. Jane is said to be the target of .his most bitter attack. Critics generally interpret his outrage against Jane, the white liberal fashioned on Gale Benson, to be the disappointment and sense of betrayal Naipaul felt, when this "nice" and "cultured" English woman "began to involve herself with Black power advocates and to work for some of the liberal causes associated with the Third World."[66] However, a look at the female characters portrayed in the early novels clearly reveals that Naipaul's antagonism is not just limited to a particular class of women, but extends to women in general. Though all Naipaul's characters are decentred human beings, there is at least one memorable male character in his Sahara-like world—Biswas in *House*. The others are treated with full sympathy, which at times even assumes a tenderness like in the case of Jimmy and Bryant in *Guerrillas*. On the other hand even in the early novels where he was simply re-creating his past experiences, Naipaul demonstrates a gender-bias. Women in the early novels are only fringe characters portrayed as no more than nags. The only prominent women characters in the early novels are Mrs. Tulsi and Shama in

House, but they are both forces working against Biswas. Mrs. Tulsi is portrayed as an autocratic matriarch, who controls the lives of those around her and mellows down only with age. Shama, on the other hand, does undergo a transformation towards the end, but it is seen more as an achievement of Biswas's than anything else. In the later novels though the women portrayed are more prominent, they are described only in terms of their sexuality. Some of the adjectives Naipaul reserves for his women characters like "rotten meat"[67] and "dirty cunt"[68] throw light on Naipaul's attitude towards women. Sandra in *Mimic* is sensual and has an obsession about her breasts; Linda in *State* is a "man-eater,"[69] Jane is "rotten meat" and Yvette in *Bend* is a person for whom a male acquaintance becomes a "habit." In other words, the women portrayed in Naipaul's novels reflect the unhealthy attitude of the author towards hıs owmen characters. However, his works do not provide any inkling as to why Naipaul treats the women in his fiction the way he does. As the collection of his letters entitled "Letters Between a Father and Son"[70] reveals, he was very close to his mother and sisters, especially his elder sister Kamla. Selwyn Cudjoe locates this aspect of Naipaul's works within the framework of psychoanalysis, which argues that all repressions are rooted in one's sexuality. The term "sexuality," interpreted in psychoanalytical terms, is not limited to mean genital activity alone, but extends to encompass all human activity. In Selwyn Cudjoe's analysis, "repressed sexuality subverts Naipaul's understanding of the nature of the subject's construction and thereby to falsify his depiction of the emerging subject in post-colonial societies."[71] Perhaps it is another version of the weak violating the weaker. It is sad that an author of Naipaul's calibre, who is also very much aware of his responsibility as a writer, should be so insensitive and banal in his attitude to this half of humanity. In a 1981 interview, Naipaul accepts that *Guerrillas* has offended a lot of people, but defends himself by saying that the "terror of that book was inevitable." In the same interview, referring to Jane's character he says that she is a "study in vanity." He even calls *Guerrillas* a "moralistic book," which has "very hard things to say about people who play at serious things, who think they can always escape, run back to their safe world."[72] But Yvette in *Bend* is as much a victim of circumstances as Salim and, unlike Jane, has no certainties of any kind. Yet, she too is subjected to an insult which is no less shocking than Jane's murder. Naipaul's women characters, portrayed at their best are the butts of comic ridicule and at their worst the objects of scatological contempt. We can only conclude that the early novels show Naipaul's biased attitude towards women which in the later novels assumes misogynistic proportions.

REFERENCES

1. Naipaul, *Guerrillas* (London: Andre Deutsch, 1975), 42.
2. Naipaul, *A Bend in the River* (Harmondsworth: Penguin, 1980), 281.
3. Hanna Wirth—Nesher, "The Curse of Marginality: Colonialism in Naipaul's *Guerrillas*," *Modern Fiction Studies* 30.3 (1984): 544.
4. Naipaul, *State*, 9.
5. Naipaul, *Bend*, 282.
6. K.I. Madhusudana Rao, "V.S. Naipaul's *Guerrillas*: A Fable of Political Innocence and Experience," *Journal of Commonwealth Literature*. 14.1 (1979): 93.
7. Naipaul, *Guerrillas*, 27.
8. Shashi Kamra, *The Novels of V.S. Naipaul* (New Delhi: Prestige, 1990), 123.
9. Naipaul, *Guerrillas*, 53.
10. *Ibid.*, 98.
11. *Ibid.*, 37.
12. *Ibid.*, 86.
13. *Ibid.*, 185.
14. Michael Neil, "Guerrillas and Gangs: Frantz Fanon and V.S. Naipaul," *Ariel* 13.4 (1982): 27.
15. Naipaul, *Guerrillas*, 204.
16. *Ibid.*, 54.
17. Hanna Wirth-Nesher, "The Curse of Marginality," 545.
18. Naipaul, *Guerrillas*, 24.
19. *Ibid.*, 34.
20. *Ibid.*, 100.
21. *Ibid.*, 55.
22. *Ibid.*, 149.
23. *Ibid.*, 57.
24. *Ibid.*, 103.
25. *Ibid.*, 57.

26. Naipaul, *Guerrillas*, 87.
27. Sashi Kamra, *The Novels of V.S. Naipaul*, 37.
28. Naipaul, foreword, India: A wounded Civilization, by Naipaul (Harmondsworth: Penguin Books, 1987), 10.
29. Naipaul, "A New King for the Congo: Mobutu and the Nihilism of Africa," *Return*, 167-95.
30. Satendra Singh, "The Immigrant Indian Experience in Literature: Trinidad and Fiji," *Awakened Conscience*, ed. C.D. Narasimhaiah (New Delhi: Sterling, 1978), 348.
31. Naipaul, *Bend*, 120.
32. Naipaul, *Return*, 188.
33. *Ibid.*, 188.
34. Naipaul, *Bend*, 51.
35. Naipaul, *Return*, 187.
36. Naipaul, *Bend*, 72.
37. *Ibid.*, 284.
38. *Ibid.*, 17.
39. *Ibid.*, 18.
40. *Ibid.*, 24.
41. *Ibid.*, 32.
42. *Ibid.*, 32-33.
43. *Ibid.*, 59.
44. *Ibid.*, 69.
45. *Ibid.*, 69.
46. *Ibid.*, 70.
47. *Ibid.*, 67.
48. *Ibid.*, 68.
49. *Ibid.*, 68.
50. *Ibid.*, 86.
51. *Ibid.*, 93.
52. *Ibid.*, 69.
53. *Ibid.*, 94.
54. *Ibid.*, 108.
55. *Ibid.*, 109-10.
56. *Ibid.*, 114.
57. *Ibid.*, 209.
58. *Ibid.*, 281-82.
59. *Ibid.*, 22.
60. *Ibid.*, 186.
61. *Ibid.*, 143.

62. Naipaul, *Bend*, 143.
63. *Ibid.*, 9.
64. Anthony Boxill, *V.S. Naipaul's Fiction*, 74.
65. Naipaul, "A conversation with V.S. Naipaul, by Bharati Mukherjee and Robert Boyers," *Salmagundi*, 54 (1981): 6.
66. Selwyn Cudjoe, *V.S. Naipaul: A Materialist Reading*, 172-73.
67. Naipaul, *Guerrilla*, 239.
68. *Ibid.*, 241.
69. Naipaul, *State*, 120.
70. Naipaul, *Letters Between a Father and Son*, (London: Abacus, 2000).
71. Selwyn Cudjoe, *V.S. Naipaul: A Materialist Reading*, 194.
72. Naipaul, "A Conversation With V.S. Naipaul," *Salmagundi* 54 (1981), 16.

6

CONCLUSION

In inquiring into the presentation of the postcolonial situation in V.S. Naipaul's novels, the aim has been to focus on the human consequences of colonialism which has been the novelist's major concern in both his fiction as well as non-fiction. The colonial experience, fraught as it was with pain, distress and anguish, has been a bitter one for the colonized. It was during colonial rule in the West Indies that the darkest crimes against humanity—genocide and slavery—were perpetrated. Some tribes that offered resistance, were completely wiped out during conquest; still others were captured and subjected to slavery.

Colonization meant not just economic exploitation but the exercising of total control over every aspect of the lives of the colonized through the subtle process of cultural colonization. The process of cultural colonization was accomplished in a sustained and systematic manner. The education provided in the colonies as well as the myths propagated by the colonizers conditioned the mindset of the colonized in such a way that they came to believe the myths about their inferiority and accept the "superiority" of the colonizers. Eventually, as the influence of Western education became stronger, they were drawn towards the colonizing culture and gradually lapsed out of their own cultural traditions. The whole purpose of Western education had been the suffusion of Western cultural norms among the colonized not for altruistic or humanistic reasons on the part of the colonizers, but in order to ensure their own selfish interests in the colonies. The intention becomes crystal clear in Thomas Babington Macaulay's "Minute on Indian Education" written in 1835. In his words the purpose of English education in India is "to form a class who may be interpreters between us and the millions whom we govern; a class of persons, Indians in blood and colour, but English in taste, in opinions, in morals and in intellect" (qtd. in Ania Loomba: 85). However, the colonizers continued to regard the colonized with contempt even after the latter became receptive to Western culture. European humanism was indeed of a curious make up.

In addition to upsetting the cultural ties of the colonized people, colonization also led to their uprooting and displacement. There was a massive transplantation of population between the colonies which separated the colonized from their native lands and forced them to accommodate themselves in alien surroundings. This shift of population between the colonies was a deliberate measure taken to make the colonial societies heterogeneous, as homogeneous ones could have posed a political threat to the colonizers. This mixing up of various peoples created grave problems both at the individual and social levels. The intense alienation and sense of homelessness that such colonized individuals experience may be ascribed to their displacement in the alien environment. On the other hand, social complications like antagonism between different races as well as miscegenation through mixed marriages have also arisen out of it. Those born out of mixed parentage find themselves in the excruciating state of betweenity. Their identities remain clouded in uncertainty because of the complex amalgam that constitutes them.

Cultural colonization accomplished what military conquest alone could not have achieved for the colonizers. It paved its way into the minds of the colonized and made them complaisant victims. This colonization of the minds maimed the psyche of the colonized in a severe way. It robbed them of all originality and instead, instilled in them a dependency complex. In fact the sense of alienation that the colonized experience and their mimicking tendency have their roots in the feeling of inferiority that was methodically ingrained in the psyche of the colonized through cultural colonization. The crippling effect of this complex manifests itself in the post-independence period in the inability of the former colonized people to stand independently on their own and in their continuing dependence on the West for ideas and technology. Intellectual as well as financial dependence of the Third World countries on the West has made them vulnerable to neocolonialism.

The relation between literature and the historical phenomenon of imperialism has been a long and intimate one. As Edward Said points out, narrative fiction has had an especially intimate association with Empire. Crucial issues related to imperialism have been reflected, debated and even decided in the narrative. It has served as a potent medium for Third World intellectuals as well, to voice their version of the experience. Such responses to the encounter that have come from the former colonized countries form the corpus of postcolonial literature, and are interesting as they carry direct first-hand experience of the encounter.

V.S. Naipaul's importance as a novelist of the colonial experience needs no reiteration. He has been able to delineate the crises of the colonized people with a precision that comes from his own experience as a displaced colonial in Trinidad. It is Naipaul's "complex-fate"[1] that in spite of being associated with no less than three societies, he has been unable to find his moorings in any of them. This has enabled him to render a fairly detached account of his experiences. This is evident in the stance he adopts while depicting postcolonial societies. While he is deeply aware of the problems created by colonialism, he is equally conscious about some negative aspects of Third World societies that have nothing to do with colonialism. This is also why he has been surrounded by controversy. On the other hand he has been lauded by critics like Said for his unrelenting commitment to truth.[2]

Though the novels of Naipaul that have been studied in relation to the presentation of the postcolonial situation, naturally fall into two phases of Naipaul's literary career on the basis of their depiction of colonial and ex-colonial societies, we find that they are distinct in some important respects. The first four novels that fall into the first phase of Naipaul's literary career, draw mainly on Naipaul's boyhood experiences and hence the autobiographical element predominates. In these novels Naipaul is simply recording his responses to the world and fulfilling the recording, function of the artist. He has not as yet begun to analyse the responses and come to any conclusions about them. The works belonging to the second phase, however, draw on Naipaul's travel writing and are analytical in approach. Naipaul has come to fresh realizations about the novel as a form of social inquiry with the purpose of imposing a vision on the world. In the works belonging to the second phase, Naipaul quests for a meaning beyond the aesthetic.

As Naipaul claims, the first four novels especially *House*, are intensely personal to him. These novels were the outcome of his efforts to come to terms with his own displacement and understand his place in the world. To Naipaul, writing is an activity that leads to self-discovery. The act of recording his ancestry helped him in establishing his home identity by imposing an order on his jumbled experiences. His major preoccupation in these novels is the disintegration of the East Indian community and the themes of mimicry and identity crisis emerge out of it. We also notice a thematic linkage between novel to novel which serves to re-create the social background of Trinidad. *Masseur* focuses on rural Trinidad, *Suffrage* deals with its multiracial aspect and *Street* completes the picture by focusing on the urban picaroon world of Port of Spain. Together, the novels upto *House* trace the social history of the East Indian community in Trinidad.

The novels throw light on the crucial role played by Western education and the American presence during the Second World War, in the cultural disintegration of the East Indians. We note that Western education created a duality in the lives of the East Indians. In Albert Memmi's analysis: "...far from preparing the adolescent to find himself completely, school creates a permanent duality in him."[3] This duality is clearly evident in the character of Ganesh who follows the traditional profession of a mystic but wears Western clothes and makes use of Western science for the spiritual cure of his clients. Naipaul brings out the positive as well as the negative effects of the influence. On the one hand we witness Ganesh's intelligent use of Western science to cure Hector, a spiritually troubled client of his, and on the other we see cultural schizophrenics like Ramlogan, who seek to legitimise their actions in both cultural frames as the need arises.

The cultural disintegration of the East Indians takes place gradually through a process of seepage and makes itself apparent in their dress codes, their food habits and their customs. Ganesh's dress contradicts his profession. The same is true of Dhaniram, the pundit in *Elvira*. In the case of language too, we see that Hindi has been so completely replaced by English that the East Indians' use the latter even while performing traditional rituals. Similarly in the matter of food habits also, it is seen that the Western alternatives have become as much a part of the East Indians' diet as the normal Indian one. In matters pertaining to religion and traditional customs as well, we find that the East Indians' have had to make compromises. In *House*, when Hari, the family pundit dies there is no one to take his place as the younger generations have received Western education and lack the training necessary to become a pundit. As there is no one to take Hari's place, Mrs. Tulsi's faith yields and she starts following Christian religious rituals.

If Western education exerted a corrosive influence on the bastions of East Indian culture from within, the Second World War acted as an external catalytic force in the process of cultural disintegration of the East Indians by boosting up the economy and ushering in modernizing forces. It is only after the arrival of Americans that Ganesh in *Masseur* and Tuttle and Govind in *House* become prosperous. Ganesh's prosperity is reflected in the complete change that comes over Leela, his wife, who begins to emulate the externals of upperclass respectability. Govind's affluence shows in his new suits and Tuttle's in the lorry he now owns. In *Street* Edward's dress and mannerisms undergo a change soon after he starts working for the Americans. In *Suffrage*, Naipaul's main intention is to show how unsuitable the borrowed institution of democracy is for multi-racial Trinidad. However, the novel demonstrates the general cultural confusion that prevails in Elvira and adds fresh insights to the theme of disintegration. We note that pecuniary gains are given priority and even traditional customs are compromised for its sake.

In *Street* and *House* Naipaul focuses on the related issue of the identity crisis of the East Indians. The identity of a people rests on their cultural moorings. However, when the very base on which identity anchors itself is destroyed, an acute identity crisis is experienced. In the overall context of the West Indies it is seen that because of the heterogeneous and fragmented nature of these societies, which are basically transplanted ones, a unitary identity becomes an impossibility. It is against such a context that the East Indians' coming into consciousness has to be viewed. At first, there is a tendency to surrender the "self" to the "other" or the colonizing culture. In the limited and mediocre environment of colonial societies the colonized often resort to mimicry. In order to escape from the mediocre environment, migration to London becomes inevitable. Ganesh in *Masseur* and the narrator in *Street* take the escape route to London. However, it is those like Biswas in *House,* who stay back and put up a struggle against the hostile environment that are finally successful in carving an authentic identity. The theme of cultural disintegration receives a detailed treatment in *House* which represents three generations of East Indians. The collapse of the Tulsi Household symbolizes the ultimate breakdown of the East Indian community.

Naipaul's early novels have been attacked by his fellow West Indian novelist, George Lamming for what is felt to be an unsympathetic portrayal of the colonized in these novels and especially in *Suffrage.* However, the presence of characters like Foam and Herbert who display noble human qualities like loyalty and tenderness makes such accusations appear groundless. Moreover, there could not have been a more sympathetic portrayal of the plight of the colonized than Naipaul has managed to convey through Biswas's character in *House.* In the case of his African characters, however, we do note a certain limitation. Naipaul is unable to portray them with the deftness with which he handles his East Indian characters. This of course is partly due to Naipaul's unfamiliarity with the Negro community and partly because of his prejudiced opinions about Africa.

After the four novels had been written, Naipaul felt the need to refresh himself by travel. In 1960 Naipaul began his travels, from which his works of non-fiction have emerged. In his non-fiction beginning with *Passage,* we find a conscious attempt to analyse his reaction about the world. There is also a new awareness about the responsibilities of a writer. Consequently, there is a marked difference in approach, tone and themes between the novels belonging to the two phases. We notice a broadening of vision as Naipaul moves outside himself and explores other cultures and societies. In his later works the familiar Naipaulian themes of alienation, identity crisis and mimicry are viewed in a broader perspective. Naipaul is at the same time preoccupied with the broader postcolonial themes of power, freedom and neocolonialism in the emergent nations of the Third World and hence these novels are intensely political.

Naipaul's primary concern in *Mimic* being the paradox of power and freedom in the ex-colonies the protagonist of this novel is an exiled politician. Singh's reflections about his failure as a politician lend insights into the social and political realities of the newly independent countries. Instead of order, there is a "controlled chaos" and Singh's government is unable to bring about anything positive partly because of their own inadequacies and partly because of deficiencies inherent to the society. Naipaul shows that in fragmented, inorganic societies that lack local expertise, development in the real sense is not possible. We note that Singh's quest for identity is much more complex because he has to redefine his position in the new socio-political framework. Nevertheless, he attains self-knowledge through the act of writing which imposes an order into his otherwise fragmented life.

In *State* Naipaul probes into the meaning of freedom. It is made explicit that freedom entails responsibilities. The colonial mentality of dependence has left the ex-colonials incapable of shouldering responsibilities. We find that none of the protagonists in *State* are at ease with their new-found freedom. On the contrary, it is experienced as a burden. In the title story of *State* Naipaul focuses on the utter chaos that prevails in an African country as internal factions war against each other to seize power. There is a strong suggestion that the Africans have reverted back to their pre-colonial "bush-life," after the withdrawal of the colonial powers. The educated Africans are made out to be ineffectual copies of their white benefactors while the others are shown to be a mindless and violent lot. Naipaul's portrayal of his African characters in a totally negative light is a serious limitation of *State*. This limitation is somewhat made up in the subsequent novels, where we find characters like Bryant, Zabeth and Ferdinand. There is a sincere attempt to analyse and understand these African characters against their complex backgrounds. However, Naipaul's basic attitude towards Africa seems to remain unchanged. In his 1981 interview with Bharati Mukherjee and Robert Boyers, he dismisses Africa as a land of bush. An examination of his women characters reveals a similar limitation. We note that in his early novels, women are mostly fringe characters cast in the mould of traditional stereotypes and though they become prominent in the later novels the focus is on their sexuality. In his novels then, women figure mainly as the butts of comic ridicule or objects of scatological contempt.

Guerrillas exposes the sham behind guerrilla movements in the newly independent colonies. Naipaul's guerrillas turn out to be decentred derelicts, who are mere puppets in the hands of those who are in real control of the island. It is clear that inorganic and fragmented societies cannot have an authentic internal source of power. Even characters like Jimmy who seem to lead guerrilla movements are in the margins of power and end up pathetically. The inauthenticity of Jimmy's so called guerrilla movement is reflected in the interior decoration of Jimmy's house, which mimicks English middle-class suburbia. In *Bend* the situation further deteriorates as nihilistic forces unleash violence in all its extremities. There is total confusion and uncertainty, as no one knows what the Bigman's plans are. On the one hand he seeks to modernize Africa and plans the Domain, while on the other he tries to revive age-old practices like the African worship of ancestors through the "cult of the mother." The Liberation army's agenda is to exterminate everyone and everything that reminds them of the Europeans. Even Ferdinand, who is basically an African has anxieties and we realize that the reversal of power following independence has left everyone unsafe. Salim's shop is taken over under the policy of radicalization and he manages to escape only because of Ferdinand's help.

Naipaul's novels throw illuminating light on the corrosive influence of colonial rule on the psyche of the colonized. The sense of insecurity that springs from the identity crisis leads to existential fears which result in psychosis. In Biswas's case it leads to a nervous breakdown while Singh and Salim nearly have one. The tainting influence of the colonial experience is visible even at the level of human relationships. Every relationship is experienced as a version of the colonial binary of Domination Vs. Subordination and precludes intimacy. Even the most apolitical relationship, the one between the sexes, is infected by it. We note an element of perversity in every sexual relationship forged in the later novels. In *Guerrillas* and *Bend* such relationships end in misogynist violence.

Naipaul's inability to identify with India makes him view the concepts of identity and the state of homelessness in a fresh perspective. The concept of identity in the later novels acquire a fluidity and homelessness begins to be viewed as a boon rather than a bane. Naipaul's disappointment with England becomes evident in the fact that England no longer features as the "promised land" of the colonized but is exposed as a place which is fast falling into dereliction. In the later novels all the sojourns in England end in disappointment. Naipaul suggests that when the world is in upheaval and exile a universal condition, the past can offer no consolation. That is why it is necessary to learn to trample on the past and live in the present.

On the whole the later novels hold out little hope for Third World countries and what emerges is a bleak, apocalyptic vision of the world. The faint glimmer of hope glimpsed at the end of *Mimic* and *State* dies out in *Guerrillas*. At the end of *Mimic*, Singh has arrived at self-knowledge and is prepared to begin life afresh, while *State* concludes with Naipauls positive gesture of involvement. In *Guerrillas* however, hope is totally withdrawn. *Guerrillas* ends in misogynist violence while *Bend* concludes with the terrifying thought that "nowhere is safe now." Of the two novels *Bend*, despite its pessimistic portrayal of Africa, concludes on a positive note with Salim rejoining the world.

Naipaul's severe indictment of postcolonial societies, both in his fiction as well as non-fiction has led critics to conclude that Naipaul is a typical "colonial Anglophile," who has aligned himself to the cultural norms and values of the West. At times t is nomenclature even seems to fit Naipaul. For instance, in his portrayal of the Africans, in *State* we detect a racist tendency. However, we see that he is equally critical of the English society. His dislike for the Africans has something to do with his personal experience in Trinidad. We know that ever since the arrival of the East Indians on the Caribbean scene, an antagonism has existed between these two races. This nevertheless is a serious limitation of Naipaul's art. However, Naipaul cannot be dismissed as a colonial Anglophile. While it is quite true that Naipaul has an admiration for the positive features of Western culture, he at the same time is very clear-sighted and emphatic about his own distance from it. In his interview with Ian Hamilton he says:

> London is my metropolitan centre; it is my commercial centre; and yet I know that it is a kind of limbo and that I am a refugee in the sense that I am always peripheral. One's concerns are not the concerns of local people.[4]

These are surely not the signs of a colonial Anglophile. A look at what exactly provokes Naipaul's criticism would make his position even clearer. His impatience is directed towards intellectual and cultural parasitism and the mimicry of the West, which are the maladies common to all the ex-colonial societies of the post-imperial world. In the early novels the same shortcomings were viewed sympathetically but in the later novels his criticism becomes markedly acidic. Perhaps it is because Naipaul realized that it requires something more vigorous than sympathy to ease the ex-colonials out of their complacent attitudes. Two contradictory statements made by Naipaul support: such a presumption. In his interview with Israel Shanker in 1971 he says: "As you grow older, you understand people a lot more; you have greater sympathy with people, you enter into them much more.[5] Seven years later we hear him saying just the opposite: "My sympathy for the defeated, the futile, the abject, the idle and the parasitic gets less and less as I grow older."[6] It is clear that Naipaul's brutal analysis of the postcolonial societies is meant as a kind of shock-treatment which he believes is necessary to pull the ex-colonials out of their complacency and make them accept responsibility for themselves because it is only then that decolonization in its real sense can become possible.

Naipaul's attitude to culture is progressive, but he cannot tolerate the Third World's blind mimicry of the West. At the same time he focuses on the shortcomings of the Third World societies which have their roots in their traditional cultures. In his analysis of India in *India: A Wounded Civilization*, he points out that the Indian concept of *Karma* is debilitating because it endorses a religious response to worldly problems. It encourages passivity and leaves no scope for social inquiry. In Naipaul's view the Indian way of perceiving is negative, because Indians "do not directly explore the world; rather, they are defined by it."[7] Naipaul holds this defect of vision to be ultimately responsible for Indian's intellectual second-ratedness. Naipaul strongly advocates Western individualism and scepticism because the first leads to active involvement and exploration of the world and the second lends the correct perspective to it. The past of the Third World countries have been brutal but harping on the past can only cause pain. That is why "the past has to be seen to be dead, or the past will kill."[8] Naipaul's philosophy is encapsulated in Salim's words in *Bend*: "The world is what it is; men who are nothing, who allow themselves to be nothing, have no place in it."

In Naipaul's analysis creativity and self-appraisal are the answers to the Third World problem of intellectual second-ratedness. In his novels, writing is seen to be an activity leading to self-knowledge. Quite a number of his protagonists have a fascination for letters. It is through the act of writing that Singh attains self-knowledge, which is a pre-requisite for an authentic consciousness. However, writing has to be guided by the spirit of analysis, otherwise, it becomes just another act of mimicry as it is in the case of Ganesh and Jimmy. Ganesh's book *101 Questions and answers on the Hindu Religion* turns out to be a "cathecism" on the Hindu religion. Jimmy, ironically enough, assumes the mask of a white woman in his novel, which only reflects his absurd fantasies. Such writing cannot lead to self-knowledge.

Naipaul claims that he has decolonized himself through the practice of writing. He observes:

> ...I've decolonized myself through the practice of writing, through what I've learned from writing, looking at the world.

> But let me also add to this I feel an enormous pain about the situation.[9]

Though for Naipaul too, like his protagonists the new-found freedom is fraught with anguish, it nevertheless is a positive movement towards a genuine Third World consciousness. Taking an overview of Naipaul's contribution to literature we may conclude that his position as a writer of international repute and universal import is assured because his works have become paradigmatic of all the twentieth century experience of deracination and exile.

REFERENCES

1. Darshan Singh Manini, "The Complex Fate of V.S. Naipaul," *Colonial Consciousness in Commonwealth Literature*, 93.
2. Edward Said, *Culture and Imperialism*, 20.
3. Albert Memmi, *The Colonizer and the Colonized*, 172.
4. Naipaul, "Without a Place," by Ian Hamilton *Critical Perspectives*, 41.
5. Naipaul, "Interview with Israel Shanker" *Critical Perspectives*, 54.
6. William Drozdiak, "Writer Without a Country," *Time*, 27 Feb. 1978: 17.
7. Naipaul, *India: A Wounded Civilization*, 103.
8. *Ibid.*, 174.
9. Naipaul, "Portrait of An Artist: What Makes Naipaul Run," by Raoul Pantin, *Caribbean Contact*, 1.6 (1973): 18.

Works Consulted

PRIMARY SOURCES

Fiction

Naipaul, V.S. *The Mystic Masseur.* London: Andre Deutsch, 1957. Harmondsworth: Penguin, 1964.

——. *The Suffrage of Elvira.* London: Andre Deutsch, 1958. Harmondsworth: Penguin, 1969.

——. *Miguel Street.* London: Andre Deutsch, 1959.

——. *A House for Mr. Biswas.* London: Andre Deutsch, 1961. Harmondsworth: Penguin, 1969.

——. *Mr. Stone and the Knight's Companion.* London: Andre Deutsch, 1963. Harmondsworth: Penguin, 1973.

——. *The Mimic Men.* London: Andre Deutsch, 1967. Harmondsworth: Penguin, 1969.

——. *A Flag on the Island.* London: Andre Deutsch, 1967. Harmondsworth: Penguin, 1969.

——. *In a Free State.* London: Andre Deutsch, 1971. Harmondsworth: Penguin, 1973.

——. *Guerrillas.* London: Andre Deutsch, 1975. Harmondsworth: Penguin, 1976.

——. *A Bend in the River.* London: Andre Deutsch 1979. Harmondsworth: Penguin, 1980.

——. *The Enigma of Arrival.* Harmondsworth: Penguin, 1987.

——. *A way in the world.* London: Minerva, 1994.

Non-Fiction

Naipaul, V.S. *The Middle Passage.* London: Andre Deutsch, 1962. Harmondsworth: Penguin, 1969.

——. *An Area of Darkness.* London: Andre Deutsch, 1964. New Delhi: Penguin, 1968.

——. *The Loss of El Dorado*. London: Andre Deutsch, 1969.

——. *The Overcrowded Barracoon and other Articles*. London: Andre Deutsch, 1972. Harmondsworth: Penguin, 1976.

——. *India: A Wounded Civilization*. London: Andre Deutsch, 1977. New Delhi: Penguin, 1979.

——. *The Return of Eva Peron With the Killings in Trinidad*. New York: Alfred A. Knopf, 1980. Harmondsworth: Penguin, 1981.

——. *Among the Believers*. London: Andre Deutsch, 1981. Harmondsworth: Penguin, 1982.

——. *Finding the Centre: Two Narratives*. London: Andre Deutsch, 1984. Harmondsworth: Penguin, 1985.

——. *A Turn in the South*. Harmondsworth: Penguin, 1989.

——. *India: A Million Mutinies Now*. London: Heinemann, 1990. London: Minerva, 1991.

Letters

Naipaul, V.S. *Letters Between a Father and Son*. London: Abacus, 1999.

Articles

Naipaul, V.S. "The Little More." *Times* 13 July 1961: 13.

——. "The Documentary Heresy." *Critical Perspectives*. Ed. R.D. Hamner. London: Heinemann, 1977: 23-25.

——. "Speaking of Writing." *Times* 2 Jan. 1964: 11.

——. "Images." *New Statesman* 24 Sep. 1965: 452-53.

——. "The Writer." *Critical Perspectives*, Ed. R.D. Hamner. London: Heinemann, 1977: 30-33.

——. "What's Wrong With Being a Snob." *Critical Perspectives*. Ed. R.D. Hamner. London: Heinemann, 1977: 34-38.

——. Foreword. *The Adventure of Gurudeva and Other Stories*. By Seepersad Naipaul. London: Andre Deutsch, 1976. 7-23.

——. "Bennett Award Acceptance Speech." *The Hudson Review* 33.4 (1980/81): 481.

——. "Writing A House for Mr. Biswas." *New York Review of Books*. 24 Nov. 1983: 22-23.

Interviews

Naipaul, V.S. "Without a Place." By Ian Hamilton. *Times Literary Supplement* 30 July 1971. 897-98.

——. "Unfurnished Entrails." By Jim Douglas Henry. *Listener* 25 Nov. 1971: 721.

——. "The Novelist V.S. Naipaul Talks to Nigel Bingham about His Childhood in Trinidad." *Listener* 7 Sep. 1972: 306.

——. "V.S. Naipaul: A Transition Interview By Adrian Rowe-Evans." *Transition* Dec. 1971. Rpt. in *Quest* [Poona] Sep.-Oct. 1972: 47-55.

——. "The Novelist V.S. Naipaul Talks About His Work to Ronald Bryden." *Listener,* 22 Mar. 1973: 367-68, 370.

——. "Portrait of An Artist: What Makes Naipaul Run." Roaul Pantin. *Caribbean Contact,* 1.6 (1973): 15, 18-19.

——. "It's Everyman for Himself: V.S. Naipaul on India." By Charles Wheeler. *Listener* 27 Oct. 1977: 535, 537.

——. "V.S. Naipaul: Man Without Society." By Shenkar Israel. *New York Times Book Review* 7 Oct. 1971. Rpt. in *Critical Perspectives on V.S. Naipaul.* Ed. R.D. Hamner. London: Heinemann, 1979: 48-53.

——. "People are Proud of Being Stupid." *Newsweek* 18 Aug. 1980: 38.

——. "V.S. Naipaul: It is Out of This Violence I've Always Written." By Mel Gussow. New York Times Book Review 16 Sep. 1984: 45-46.

——. "India Has Vitality." By Rahul Singh. *India Today* 31 July 1989: 120.

——. "Delivering the Truth. "*Times Literary Supplement* 2 Sep. 1994: 3-4.

SECONDARY SOURCES

Books

Amur, G.S. and S.K. Desai, eds. *Colonial Consciousness in Commonwealth Literature.* Bombay: Somaya Publications. 1984.

Asad, Talal. Ed. *Anthropology and the Colonial Encounter.* London: Ithaca Press, 1973.

Ashcroft, Bill, Gareth Griffiths and Helen Tiffin, eds. *The Post-colonial Studies Reader*. London and New York: Routledge, 1995.

Barker, F., P. Hulme and M. Iversen. eds. *Colonial Discourse/ Post-colonial Theory*. Manchester and New York: Manchester University Press, 1994.

Bhat, Yashoda. *V.S. Naipaul: An Introduction*. New World Literature Series. Delhi: B.R. Publishing Corporation, 1999.

Boehmer, Elleke. *Colonial and Post-colonial Literature: Migrant Metaphors*. Oxford: Oxford University Press, 1995.

Boxill, Anthony, *V.S. Naipaul's Fiction: In Quest of the Enemy*. Frederiction, New Brunswick: York Press, 1983.

Cesaire, Aime. *Discourse on Colonialism*. New York: Monthly Review Press, 1972.

Childs, Peter and R.J. Patrick Williams. *An Introduction to Post-Colonial Theory*. London: Prentice Hall, 1977.

Cohn, Bernard S. *Colonialism and Its Forms of Knowledge: The British in India*. Delhi: Oxford University Press, 1997.

Cudjoe, Selwyn, R. *V.S. Naipaul: A Materialist Reading*. Amherst: The University of Massachusetts Press, 1988.

Eagleton, Terry. *Exiles and Emigres*. London: Chatto and Windus, 1970.

——. *Black Skin, White Masks*. 1952. London: Pluto Press, 1986.

——. *Studies in a Dying Colonialism*. 1959. Harmondsworth: Penguin, 1970.

——. *The Wretched of the Earth*. 1961. Harmondsworth: Penguin, 1971.

Friedl, John and John E. Pfeiffer. *Anthropology*: The Study of People. New York: Harper and Row, 1977.

Goonatilake, Sushanta. *Crippled Minds: An Exploration into Colonial Culture*. Bombay: Vikas, 1982.

Gowda, Anniah H.H. ed. *The Colonial and Neo-Colonial Encounters in Commonwealth Literature*. Mysore: Mysore University Press, 1983.

Green, Martin. *Dreams of Adventure, Deeds of Empire*. London: Routledge and Kegan Paul, 1979.

Gurr, Andrew. *Writers in Exile: The Creative use of Home in Modern Literature.* Sussex: The Harvester Press, 1981.

Hamner, R.D. ed. *Critical Perspectives on V.S. Naipaul.* London: Heinemann, 1979.

Hayman, Ronald. *The Novel Today,* 1967-75. Harlow: Longman, 1976.

Hermassi, Elbaki. *The Third World Reassessed.* Berkeley: University of California Press, 1980.

Hughes, Peter. *V.S. Naipaul.* Contemporary Writers. London: Routledge, 1988.

Joshi, Chandra B. *V.S. Naipaul: The Voice of Exile.* Delhi: Sterling Publishers, 1994.

Kamra, Sashi. *The Novels of V.S. Naipaul.* New Delhi: Prestige, 1990.

Kiernan, V.G. *Marxism and Imperialism.* New York: St. Martins Press, 1974.

King, Bruce, ed. *Literatures of the World in English.* London: Routledge, 1974.

——. *West Indian Literature.* London: Macmillan, 1979.

——. V.S. Naipaul. *Macmillan Modern Novelists,* London: Macmillan, 1993.

Lamming, George. *In the Castle of My Skin.* 1953. London: Longman Drumbeat, 1979.

——. *The Pleasures of Exile.* London: Michael Joseph, 1960.

Loomba, Ania. *Colonialism/Post-colonialism.* London: Routledge, 1998.

Mahood, M.M. *The Colonial Encounter.* London: Rex Collings, 1977.

Memmi, Albert. *The Colonizer and the Colonized,* London: Earthscan, 1990.

Moore, Gerald. *The Chosen Tongue: English Writing in the Tropical World.* London: Longman, 1969.

Mustafa, Fawzia. *V.S. Naipaul.* Cambridge Studies in African and Caribbean Literature. Cambridge: Cambridge University Press, 1995.

Naipaul, Seepersad. *The Adventures of Gurudeva and other Stories*. London: Andre Deutsch, 1976.

Nandy, Ashis. *The Intimate Ememy: Loss and Recovery of Self under Colonialism*. Delhi: Oxford University Press, 1983.

Narasimhaiah, C.D. ed. *Awakened Conscience: Studies in Commonwealth Literature*. New Delhi: Sterling, 1978.

——. *The Critical Indian Scene: Controversial Essays*. Delhi: B.R. Publishing House, 1990.

Newson, Linda A. *Aboriginal and Spanish Colonial Trinidad: A Study in Culture Contact*. London: Academic Press, 1976.

Nixon, Rob. *V.S. Naipaul: Postcolonial Mandarin*. Oxford: Oxford University Press, 1992.

Rai, Sudha. *V.S. Naipaul: A Study in Expatriate Sensibility*. New Delhi: Arnold Heinemann, 1982.

Ramadevi, N. *The Novels of V.S. Naipaul: Quest for order and Identity*. New Delhi: Prestige, 1996.

Ramchand, Kenneth. *The West Indian Novel and its Background*. London: Faber and Faber, 1970.

Rao, Madhusudana K.I. *Contrary Awareness: A Critical Study of the Novel of V.S. Naipaul*. Guntur: Saradhi, 1982.

Said, Edward. *Orientalism*. London: Routledge and Kegan Paul. 1978.

——. *Culture and Imperialism*. 1993. London: Vintage, 1994.

Singh, Manjit Inder. *V.S. Naipaul: Writers of the Indian Diaspora*. Jaipur: Rawat Publications, 1998.

Snyder, Louis L. ed. *The Imperialism Reader: Documents and Readings on Modern Expansionism*. New York: D. Van Nostrand Company, 1962.

Suleri, Sara. *The Rhetoric of English in India*. Chicago: University of Chicago Press, 1992.

Swinden, Patrick. *The English Novel of History and Society, 1940-80*. London: Macmillan, 1984.

Theroux, Paul. *V.S. Naipaul: An Introduction to His Work*. London: Andre Deutsch, 1972.

Thorpe, Michael. *V.S. Naipaul*. London: British Council Longman, 1976.

Tomllinson, John. *Cultural Imperialism.* London: Pinter, 1991.

Walsh, William. "*V.S. Naipaul.* The Modern Writers" Series. Edinburgh: Oliver and Boyd, 1973.

——. ed. *A Manifold Voice: Studies in Commonwealth Literature.* London: Chatto and Windus, 1970.

——. ed. *Readings in Commonwealth Literature.* Oxford: The Clarendon Press, 1973.

Williams, Eric. *History of the People of Trinidad and Tabago.* London: Andre Deutsch, 1964.

——. *From Columbus to Castro: The History of the Caribbean, 1492-1967.* London: Andre Deutsch, 1970.

Articles

Anderson, Linda R. "Ideas of Identity and Freedom in V.S. Naipaul and Joseph Conrad." *English Studies,* 59 (1978): 510-17.

Angrosino, M.B. "V.S. Naipaul and the Colonial Image." *Caribbean Quarterly* 21.3 (1975): 1-11.

Belitt, Ben. "The Heraldry of Accommodation: A House for Mr. Naipaul." *Salmagundi.* 54 (1981): 22-24.

Birje-Patil J. "From Heart of Darkness to a Free State." *Colonial Consciousness in Commonwealth Literature.* eds. G.S. Amur and S.K. Desai. 110-18.

Blaise, Clark. "The Commonwealth Writers and His Material." *Awakened Conscience: Studies in Commonwealth Literature.* Ed. C.D. Narsimhaiah. New Delhi: Sterling, 1978. 118-26.

Boxill, Anthony. "V.S. Naipaul's Starting Point." *Journal of Commonwealth Literature.* 10.1 (1975): 1-9.

——. "Mr. Biswas, Mr. Polly and the Problem of V.S. Naipaul's Sources." *Ariel,* 8.3 (1977): 129-41.

Carthew, John. "Adapting to Trinidad: Mr. Biswas and Mr. Polly Revisited." *Journal of Commonwealth Literature,* 13.1 (1978): 58-64.

Cooke, John. "A Vision of the Land: V.S. Naipaul's later Novels." *Caribbean Quarterly.* 25.4 (1979): 31-47.

Derrick, A.C. "Naipaul's technique as a Novelist." *Critical Perspectives,* ed. Hamner. 194-206.

Drozdiak, William. "Writer Without a Country." *Time* 27 Feb. 1978.

Fido, Martin. "Mr. Biswas and Mr. Polly." *Ariel* 5.4 (1974): 30-37.

Garebian, Keith. "V.S. Naipaul's Negative Sense of Place." *Journal of Commonwealth Literature.* 10.1 (1975): 23-25.

——. "The Grotesque Satire of *A House for Mr. Biswas. Modern Fiction Studies: Special Number on V.S. Naipaul.* 30.3 (1984): 487-96.

Goodheart, Eugene. "V.S. Naipaul's Mandarin Sensibility." *Partisan Review* 50.2 (1983): 244-56.

Gowda, H.H. Anniah. "Naipaul in India." *Literary Half Yearly* 11.2 (1970): 163-70.

Gurr, Andrew. "The Freedom of Exile in Naipaul and Doris Lessing." *Ariel* 13.4 (1982): 8-18.

Hamner, R.D. "Character and Setting." *Critical Perspectives.* Ed. Hamner. 205-41.

King, Bruce. "Recent Commonwealth Fiction." *Sewanee Review.* 85 (1977): 126-34.

Krikler, Bernard. "V.S. Naipaul's *A House for Mr. Biswas.*" *Listener* 13 Feb. 1964: 270-71.

Langran, Phillip. "V.S. Naipaul: A Question of Detachment." *Journal of Commonwealth Literature.* 25.1 (1990): 133-41.

Lazarus, Neil. "National Consciousness and Intellectualism." *Colonial Discourse/ Postcolonial theory,* eds. Barker, Hulme and Iversen. 197-220.

Lee, R.H. "The Novels of V.S. Naipaul." *Critical Perspectives,* Ed. Hamner. 68-83.

Lindroth, James R. "The Figure of Performance in Naipaul's *The Mimic Men. Modern Fiction Studies: Special Number on V.S. Naipaul.* 30.3 (1984): 519-29.

MacDonald, Bruce F. "Symbolic Action in Three of V.S. Naipaul's Novel." *Critical Perspectives,* Ed. Hamner. 242-54.

——. "The Birth of Mr. Biswas." *Journal of Commonwealth Literature* 11.3 (1977): 50-54.

Maini, Darshan Singh. "The Complex Fate of V.S. Naipual."

Colonial Consciousness in Commonwealth Literature. Eds. G.S. Amur and S.K. Desai. 93-109.

Mann, Harveen Sachdeva. "Variations on the theme of Mimicry: Naipaul's *The Mystic Masseur* and *The Suffrage of Elvira.*" *Modern Fiction Studies.* 30.3 (1984): 467-85.

Michener, Charles. "The Dark Visions of V. S. Naipaul." *Newsweek* 16 Nov. 1981: 104-15.

Miller, Karl. "Naipaul's Emergent Country." *The Listener* 28 Sep. 1967: 402-3.

——. "V.S. Naipaul and the New order." *Critical Perspectives,* Ed. Hamner. 111-25.

Moore, Gerald. "East Indians West: The Novels of V.S. Naipaul." *Black Orpheus* 7 June (1960): 11-15.

Mukherjee, Meenakshi. "Caliban's Growth: Impact of Colonialism on Commonwealth Fiction." *Colonial Consciousness in Commonwealth Literature* ed. G.S. Amur and S.K. Desai. 216-227.

Nachman, Larry David. "The Worlds of V.S. Naipaul." *Salmagundi* 54 (1981): 59-76.

Nazareth, Peter. "The Mimic Men as a Study of Corruption. Critical Perspectives Ed. Hamner, 137-52.

Neill, Michael. "Guerrillas and Gangs: Frantz Fanon and V.S. Naipaul." *Ariel* 13.4 (1982): 21-62.

Ormerod, David. "In a Derelict Land: The Novels of V.S. Naipaul. *Critical Perspectives* Ed. Hamner. 159-77.

Padhi, Bibhu. "Naipaul on Naipaul and the Novel." *Modern Fiction Studies* 30.3 (1984): 455-65.

Parrinder, Patrick. "V.S. Naipaul and the Uses of Literacy." *Critical Quarterly* 21.2 (1979): 5-13.

Prescott, Lynda. "Past and Present Darkness: Sources for V.S. Naipaul's *A Bend in the River.*" *Modern Fiction Studies* 30.3 (1984): 547-59.

Pritchett, V.S. "Climacteric" *Critical Perspectives* Ed. Hamner: 104-10.

Ramraj, Victor. "The All-Embracing Christ like vision: Tone and Attitude in *The Mimic Men.*" *Critical Perspectives* Ed. Hamner: 127-35.

Rao, K.I. Madhusudana. "V.S. Naipaul's Guerrillas:" A Fable of Political Innocence and Experience. *Journal of Commonwealth Literature.* 14.1 (1979): 90-99.

Rohlehr, Gordon. "The Ironic Approach: The Novels of V.S. Naipaul." *Critical Perspectives* Ed. Hamner. 178-93.

——. "Character and Rebellion in *A House for Mr. Biswas.* New World Quarterly 4.4 (1968): 66-72.

Sharpe, Jenny. "Figures of Colonial Resistance." *Modern Fiction Studies* 35.1 (1989): 137-79.

Srinath, C.N. "Crisis of Identity: Assertion and Withdrawal in Naipaul and Arun Joshi." *Literary Criterion* 14.1 (1979): 33-41.

Theroux, Paul. "V.S. Naipaul." *Modern Fiction Studies.* 30.3 (1984): 339-43.

Thieme, John. "V.S. Naipaul's Third World: A Not So Free State." *Journal of Commonwealth Literature* 10.1 (1975): 10-22.

——. "A Hindu Castaway: Ralph Singh's Journey in *The Mimic Men.*" *Modern Fiction Studies* 30.3 (1984): 505-15.

Walsh, William. "V.S. Naipaul: Mr. Biswas." *Literary Criterion* 10.2 (1972): 27-37.

Warner-Lewis, Maureen. "Cultural Confrontation, Disintegration and syncretism in *A House for Mr. Biswas.*" *Critical Perspectives,* 94-103.

Wirth-Nesher, Hana. "The Curse of Marginality Colonialism in Naipaul's *Guerrillas.*" *Modern Fiction Studies,* 30.3 (1984): 531-45.

Woodcock, Bruce. "Post-1975 Caribbean Fiction and the Challenge to English Literature." *Critical Quarterly* 28.4 (1986): 79-95.

Woodcock, George. "Two Great Commonwealth Novelists: R.K. Narayan and V.S. Naipaul." *Sewanee Review* 87 (1979): 1-28.

Index